THE WHITE HOUSE
GARDEN
WILLIAM SEALE

WITH PHOTOGRAPHS BY ERIK KVALSVIK

WHITE HOUSE HISTORICAL ASSOCIATION · WASHINGTON, D.C.

This book is for Irvin Martin Williams,
Superintendent of Grounds for the White House

WHITE HOUSE HISTORICAL ASSOCIATION

A nonprofit organization, chartered on November 3, 1961, to enhance
understanding, appreciation, and enjoyment of the Executive Mansion.
Income from the sale of this book will be used to publish other
materials about the White House as well as to acquire historic
furnishings and other objects for the Executive Mansion. Address
inquiries to 740 Jackson Place, N.W., Washington, D.C. 20503-0300.

EXECUTIVE VICE PRESIDENT: Neil W. Horstman
DIRECTOR OF PUBLICATIONS: Donald J. Crump

Copyright © 1996 White House Historical Association

The National Geographic Society supervised the production, printing,
and binding of this book as a public service.

LIBRARY OF CONGRESS CATALOG CARD NUMBER 96-079736
ISBN 0-912308-69-9 (casebound)
Second Edition, 1996

Produced by Archetype Press, Inc., Washington, D.C.
Diane Maddex, *Project Director*
Robert L. Wiser, *Designer*

Contents

The White House gardens are a genuine treasure. Their year-round beauty brings joy to millions of Americans, both inside and outside the White House. But like the wonderful old house they surround, these grounds and gardens also stand for something larger. They capture the magnificence and diversity of the American landscape. And they remind us of our proud past. Nearly every tree represents a President. At the White House are magnolias planted by Franklin D. Roosevelt and John F. Kennedy, oaks brought in by Dwight D. Eisenhower and Ronald Reagan, an American boxwood from Harry S. Truman. Like the Presidents whose values and ideals they honor, these trees are rooted in our very soil.

Beneath the limbs of these trees, generations of Americans have had the opportunity to gather on the green, rolling lawns of the White House—for picnics and Easter egg rolling, treaty signings, and ceremonies honoring the accomplishments of our fellow citizens. It seems only natural that Americans have used this place to come together. After all, just as the White House is the "People's House," its garden is truly America's garden.

This book tells the story of the White House garden—its trees, its plants, its history. I hope that everyone who reads it will come away with renewed admiration for a garden that is a proud tribute to the great country it represents.

William Jefferson Clinton

Introduction

The land now occupied by the White House garden was being cultivated nearly four hundred years ago, when Capt. John Smith saw from his ship the long ridge that sloped south to marshes along the Potomac River. It then belonged to the Algonquin and Nacotchtankes tribes, who were farmers and hunters. By the time of the American Revolution, English colonial planters, in possession for five generations, had divided it up and laid it waste planting tobacco.

In 1790 the site was an obscure spot in the federal district set aside for the national capital. Less than a year later it took on its historic role. On November 1, 2000, the garden will have served the presidency for two centuries.

Much is said about the interiors of the White House, but the personal affections of the Presidents and their families more often center in the grounds. Retreating here, they find everyday pleasures. Some have even been gardeners.

The President's Park, established in 1791, is the official designation of the eighty-two acres whose centerpiece is the White House. It includes Lafayette Park on the north and the Ellipse on the south. The immediate grounds of the White House are a smaller part of the park, contained within an iron fence and entered through iron gates.

The White House garden began with big ideas. Located within the gardenlike plan of the capital itself, the President's Park was larger than most American farms. George Washington delighted in the magnificent conception of broad avenues slashing a grid of lesser streets at angles, connecting public buildings of huge scale and variety, pools and forests, lawns and monuments—nature everywhere enhanced by formal order.

The White House garden has become a green refuge from the paved-over heart of the capital. Plant material grows lush, unrestrained by civilization all around. Wild birds nest in the trees and bathe in the fountains, oblivious to presidential security. People, on the other hand, are restricted largely to postcard views of the grounds from Lafayette Park and the Ellipse. This book shows the White House garden as you might see it today if you, like the wild birds, could enter and wander at will.

Tree planting at the White House began during Andrew Jackson's administration in the 1830s and has never really stopped. This prized Magnolia grandiflora *on the south side of the White House is part of the Jackson legacy.*

A Day in the White House Garden

Sunny 'Daisy goal' and 'Tolima' chrysanthemums are planted en masse for fall (top), while American boxwood hedges border yellow and white mums in the Rose Garden, with crab apple trees overhead (opposite).

The garden's day begins quietly at sunup, when the tranquillity of the White House is its wonder. Daylight illuminates the far vistas of monuments, river, and parks and penetrates the closer, deep shadows of the thick plantings of trees and the sheltered gardens near the President's House. On any given day the walls of the building itself are likely to take on an orange or pink or lilac iridescence, briefly, before the white asserts itself. By 7:00 a.m., when the first human presence appears, all is light and in order.

On this late spring morning a green truck grinds through the Southwest Gate. Six men in jump suits sit atop a pile of mulch; they laugh and joke, but in voices so low that they are not heard over the motor's quiet hum. They stop at a spot for which plans have been made a season in advance.

The workmen are planting a flower bed for summer. The long, broad bed wraps around the south fountain and is edged by a carpet of close-clipped lawn. Its bounty of flowers has turned from red to brindle in the hot sun.

The men jump down and swarm, ruthlessly pulling from the black soil the nodding heads of wilting red tulips that for weeks have made such a show. The outcast bulbs are piled on the truck, and the workers take to the dirt with their shovels, chopping it finely and spreading a snowy nutrient, which they work into the soil so that the white finally disappears into the black.

Most of the soil in the White House flower beds is rich in nutrients as well as earthworms. Practically anything will grow, although Washington's is an inconstant climate: too far north for many southern plants and too far south for many northern plants. Fertilizing by the clock helps ensure the new display of flowers to come. The White House tends to be intolerant of poor shows.

A smaller truck stops in the Rose Garden with trays of seedlings to be planted. Here are summer asters, daisies, phlox, black-eyed Susans, candytuft, mullein, coral-bells, all old-fashioned flowers massed together to rise by late June in floral abundance that will last until the first frost in October. Then, they too will be pulled out and replaced by chrysanthemums, overplanted with pansies that will dominate the bed for the winter. Years of trial and error have made the White House garden one of extraordinary variety.

The gardeners, finished in a mere three hours, clean up the areas and vanish with their trucks. The only evidence that they were there is visible mainly to other gardeners. ❧

THE

GARDEN GROWS

The President's Park

When the U.S. Constitution was new, the Federal government, seated in New York, debated where to locate the permanent capital. President George Washington worked behind the scenes with Thomas Jefferson and James Madison, politicking Congress to favor a certain place in the South, on the Potomac River. Washington envisioned the Potomac as a golden artery of commerce between the rich frontier and the sea. It would nurture the city to greatness.

He had his way in 1790. The new city was designated by law to rise more or less in the center of the United States, in a sparsely populated, rural area on the Potomac that owed no homage to northern money. Congress placed the ten-square-mile Federal District of Columbia on land ceded by Maryland and Virginia. The capital was to be occupied in ten years—1800—and the details of building it were left to the President.

Between the fall of 1791 and the end of 1792, Washington formulated ideas for the look of the capital. He wanted it to be like Paris or London, serving as both the government and the business center of the country. His politics anticipated big government, a future America that would sit at the diplomatic tables as an equal with the mightiest kingdoms of Europe. Whatever else the new city might be, it must be appropriate to the augustness of a New World empire.

To draw his city design, he selected a man he greatly admired: Pierre Charles L'Enfant, a native of France who had shed his blood in the War of Independence and had stayed on to design pageants, dinners, and parades that had helped promote the Constitution. L'Enfant, an artist and a military engineer to some extent, gave heart and soul to the work and was able to spread a plan before the President in the fall of 1791.

The proposal recalled the ceremonial grandeur of France in the recent, vanished days of absolute monarchy and incorporated ideas of city planning that had been current in Europe for the preceding forty years. In plan the city looked like a formal garden. Central to it, in a park of eighty-two acres, stood the presidential "palace," approached on the north by radial avenues; gardens extended to the south, where terraces dropped off to pools and a vista through a dense woodland framed a distant pyramid.

An early (ca. 1825) watercolor of the White House from the southwest (preceding pages) shows Jefferson's stone wall, workers' cottages, and the South Portico built for James Monroe in 1824. From atop the South Portico today (opposite), the capital city envisioned two centuries ago by George Washington and Pierre Charles L'Enfant spreads to the southeast.

While the most imaginative details never materialized, the plan set the boundaries of the President's Park. Washington approved nearly everything that L'Enfant suggested, but he amended at least one feature by rejecting the site first proposed for the residence, moving it instead slightly southward, perhaps to take fuller advantage of the panoramic view.

Washington, D.C., was built generally as L'Enfant had drawn it. The Frenchman's scheme for a palace was cast out in favor of a smaller presidential mansion, designed by the Irish-born and -trained James Hoban. His model was Leinster House in Dublin, a stately house then nearly fifty years old. The resulting design, modified by George Washington, is the White House we know.

In the summer of 1792 the President himself sited the house. Raw stakes and string outlined a rectangle with a southward semicircle that the Blue Room would one day occupy. The President's House straddled the slope of a ridge that divided the upper (northern) and lower (southern) parts of the President's Park. It was an immense house by American standards—the largest in the country—but Hoban's mansion was only one-fourth the size of the palace that Washington first approved.

Even for George Washington, a farmer and horticulturist, it took imagination to envision much elegance in the presidential landscape. The tract had once been part of Maryland. Its southern extremity was low and watery, fringed with cattails and marsh grasses, edging up to the perilous waters of Tiber Creek that beat a swift path to the Potomac. From the Tiber the President's Park rose northward, sloping to a ridge some forty feet above its starting point.

The high elevation of the ridge divided the park, as it did the city, into hill and plain. From the south the ridge seemed smaller than it was, but from on top of it, looking back to the south, Maryland and Virginia spread before the eye for miles, crisscrossed by shaggy fence rows, shadowed by deep forests, sparkling when the sun reflected in the river and creeks. The view was spectacular then and is now, two centuries later, even in the environs of a city. From the windows of his private living quarters upstairs, the President can still enjoy one of the finest prospects in the United States.

President Washington hurried the government's acquisition of land. The area between the ridge and Tiber Creek, today's South Grounds, belonged to a tight-fisted tobacco planter, Davy Burns, who held out for a higher price than the city commissioners had hoped to pay. Washington personally intervened,

L'Enfant's 1792 plan for the city of Washington (above) called for radial avenues leading to the north entrance of the President's House, but these were only partially built and now converge on Lafayette Park instead (opposite). The plan, accepted by George Washington, projected a mansion four times the size of the White House with terraced gardens to the south.

reasoning with Burns that the land was too wet to farm and thus should not command much; but Burns recognized a seller's market and stood pat. The President accused Burns of blocking progress. Burns countered that profit of course meant little to Washington, because he had married a rich widow. The President ultimately lost the battle, paid the price, and the White House got its back yard.

On the north side of the President's Park, up on the ridge where the house was rising and beyond, the land stretched back, falling some but giving the impression of a relatively level area. This was a plantation known as Jamaica, once a prosperous enterprise in the colonial heyday of Maryland tobacco. Ghosts of furrows ran up to the old Pierce cottage, which nestled among ancient apple trees that still bloomed in May. Large hardwood shade trees, intermingled there, had never yielded their ground to tobacco fields.

Pierces had lived in the small farmhouse for nearly a century, burying their dead within its yard fence. They left abruptly, as with the wind, selling out to Sam Davidson, a Philadelphia developer who had learned the location of the President's palace. Davidson almost immediately sold the farm to the government, but he was to claim parts of the President's North Grounds in litigation that ran for nearly twenty years. As it turned out, the Pierce farm was to be largely covered by paved streets north of the White House. The planted grounds of the mansion, for the most part, would be on Davy Burns's costly marshes to the south.

Some believed the President's Park to be too large. Even as

Scottish stonemasons in the 1790s framed the North Entrance of the White House (opposite) in a garden of their own, carved in Aquia sandstone: garlands of oak leaves and acorns, mingled with roses and acanthus leaves. Real roses, such as these 'Icebergs' (below), have long since grown in the Rose Garden.

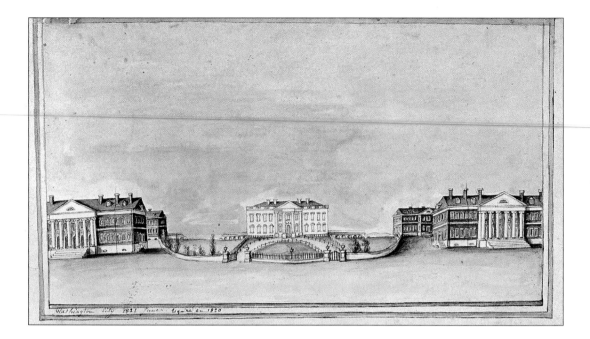

Anne-Marguerite Hyde de Neuville, wife of the French minister to the United States, painted the White House and the second set of department office buildings from the north (above) in 1820. An aged beech tree planted before 1900 (opposite) shields the west facade of the Treasury Department—the third version on this site—which by 1871 had entirely replaced the two Federal office buildings depicted at the left of Hyde de Neuville's watercolor.

the dressed stone walls of the house took form, the city commissioners suggested subdividing the kingly sprawl of park, the "gloomy wilderness," into smaller, more republican parcels. Washington would not surrender an inch. Instead, he wanted to plant a "botanical garden," the perfect setting for an official residence. Haste and diminishing time made him lay that aside, just as he did the terraces, pools, pyramid, and radial streets.

But the eighty-two acres of the President's Park survived intact. In the winter of 1797, just before his retirement, Washington himself made the first permanent intrusion by establishing public office buildings within its bounds, one on each side of the President's House. He had yielded to politics. The architectural descendants of these early red brick structures stand on the east—the Treasury Department, built 1836–71—and on the west, the Old Executive Office Building (Old State, War, and Navy), built 1871–88. Each is only the third building on its site.

Further subdivision of the President's Park was to take place after Washington's time. Within twenty-five years Lafayette Park was partitioned off the northern end, and it was separated entirely when Pennsylvania Avenue was cut through in 1822. The White House was by that time fenced away from most of the marsh to the south, which forms today's Ellipse. Yet the entire President's Park, including the Ellipse and Lafayette Park, still survives as an official entity and constitutes the official domain of the White House.

Evolution
of the
President's
Park

Based on old documents, plans, and maps, these modern renditions show the President's Park in four periods of its history: 1800 (above left), 1860 (above right), 1900 (opposite left), and 1990 (opposite right).

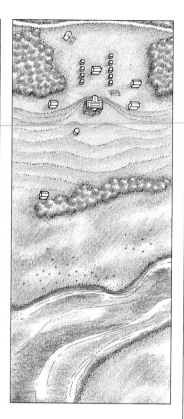

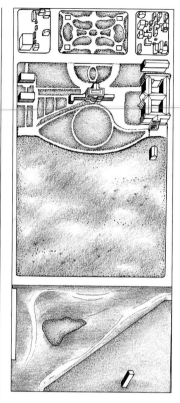

Four significant periods mark the evolution of the White House grounds and the President's Park over the past two centuries. In 1800, the year the mansion was first occupied, the terrain was little changed from the farmland and wilderness that George Washington and Pierre L'Enfant found here. On its ridge the new house, white-washed by its builders, over-looked a sloping sprawl of meadow to the south, termi-nating in a large marsh that ran to Tiber Creek and the Potomac River.

On the eve of the Civil War sixty years later, the White House grounds, reduced in acreage by Thomas Jefferson, were smaller still with the sur-

render of the sites of the for-mal garden and the orangery to the Treasury expansion on the east. Jefferson's stone wall fenced the south and west, and James Monroe's iron pickets bounded the north. The arch-of-triumph gate from Pennsylvania Avenue on the southeast, rendered obsolete, was being demol-ished. Expansion of the Treasury Building was almost complete, with the Navy and War Departments still occupy-ing their early red brick office buildings on the west.

By 1900 the marsh had been drained and filled and the South Grounds extended into it by Ulysses S. Grant, raising the level seven to ten feet. Beyond the curving south

fence the Ellipse, laid out by Rutherford B. Hayes, and a network of drives led to the Washington Monument, completed in 1884. The vast new State, War and Navy Building rose on the west.

The arrangement of the park in the 1990s is somewhat the same, except for the closing of Pennsylvania Avenue to automobile traffic. Wings have enlarged the house, and the usual entrance is on the east side. The iron fence still forms a semicircle on the south, while the Ellipse remains open parkland. Perhaps the main difference in the 1990s is restrictions on use of the grounds, a result of the tightening of security that has taken place since World War II. ❧

Seeds
of Hope

George Washington apparently never planted a seed or root at the White House. That honor he left to his successors. The first of these, John Adams, followed him in office while the capital was still in Philadelphia. A learned man, and an often unpopular President eager to please, Adams listened to criticisms of Washington's city after the general's death in 1799 and even entertained the idea of living in a rowhouse near the Capitol and giving the White House over to the Supreme Court.

As the legal date to occupy the city approached, he changed his mind and duly obeyed the Residence Act of 1790 by moving into the White House on the first day of November 1800. For nearly a year before, he frequently thought about the new house and its garden. In January 1800 Secretary of the Navy Benjamin Stoddert had already written to William Thornton, the architect of the Capitol and one of the city commissioners, that "something like a garden on the north side of the President's House" would "give the president and Mrs. Adams great satisfaction." He reminded Thornton of the Philadelphia garden of William Bingham between Third and Fourth Streets, done in the picturesque English style universally admired. "The ground should not be levelled," wrote the secretary, urging that tree planting begin "at once."

Adams's own gardening concerns were more pragmatic. While living in Philadelphia, and burdened with the high expenses of maintaining a hospitable presidential house, he became concerned that the cost of entertaining in Washington would ruin him. Abigail Smith Adams reminded him that George Washington had been a rich man; Adams was not. All his official expenses had to be covered by his salary of $25,000 a year, a fantastic amount to the average citizen. But average citizens did not have to feed thirty people at table every day.

The President, who was standing for reelection, wanted a vegetable garden plowed and fertilized, with the optimistic goal of planting it in the early spring. In the fall of 1800 Thornton accordingly created such a garden, probably on a level place northeast of the White House, where Pennsylvania Avenue now crosses. But when time came for sowing seeds in the spring,

A view from the south underscores the tremendous variety in the grade of the White House grounds. Here the land rises in swells, most of which have been created by fill over two centuries.

Adams was already back home in Quincy, Massachusetts, returned to private life by the triumphant Thomas Jefferson.

John Adams's garden was not the first White House project to be terminated by political bad luck. Thornton did make plans for a pleasure garden for the President, but when Jefferson's "revolution of 1800" took place the Federalist Age ended. All plans were scrapped, and Thornton's are lost.

In the blaze of a new vision for America, the Republican Thomas Jefferson moved to the White House in March 1801, eager to make his own mark. The house, although to Jefferson's eye archaic, was already built, but the grounds offered plenty of opportunity for change. Construction litter covered the park; brick kilns, now cold, were still in place. A survey conducted by the commissioners of the Federal city in the fall of 1801 recorded twenty-two buildings in the President's Park, including "1 house of stone. 6 of brick. 15 of wood." The stone house we know. The brick structures included the two Federal office buildings and perhaps the Pierce farmhouse and some other former residences or outbuildings. Certainly most of the fifteen wooden buildings were workers' cottages, the last of which would not be auctioned off and rolled away until 1804.

Jefferson's several architectural alterations to the White House, notably his design in about 1804 and partial construction in 1807 and 1808 of the East and West Colonnades, are well known, but it was his work on the grounds that occupied his attention all his eight years in office. A farmer himself with a strong personal interest in plants, Jefferson kept gardening notebooks in which he recorded observations of all kinds about vegetables, flowers, fruits, and trees. One of his White House gardens was in his office, the current State Dining

A monumental gate (above), painted by Anne-Marguerite Hyde de Neuville about 1820, stood at the Southeast Entrance and can be seen in the lower right of Thomas Jefferson's drawing of the White House grounds (right). Dating from about 1802–5, the sketch appears to be in Jefferson's hand and represents the ideas that drove most gardening at the White House for more than fifty years.

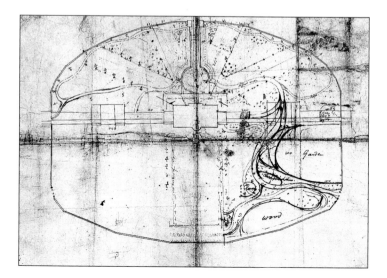

Room, where in pots and boxes in the three sunny window recesses on the south he cultivated geraniums, strawberries, figs, and orange trees.

Jefferson faced a landscape used but also abused. Many of the stately old native trees in the park had fallen for firewood before the axes of trespassers. Republicans were sure that bitter Federalists had done the deed as an affront to the victors of 1800. The stump-dotted red earth looked like a battleground, filled with holes and debris. The President tackled the problem of a White House landscape as he might address the subject for his own house, the difference being that the White House was symbolic of the presidency and not himself personally.

First with homely split rails, but with plans for permanent stone walls, he enclosed perhaps eight acres around the mansion, throwing most of the remaining seventy-four into other use or disuse. A high wall of common stone was built around the south end of the grounds in 1808, but Jefferson's plan to enclose the entire property with walls was to be realized only after his presidency.

Although a road separated the South Grounds of the house from the field and marshes leading to Tiber Creek—giving local traffic headed for Georgetown a shortcut—Pennsylvania Avenue did not yet cross on the north. Jefferson used his rail fence to divide off a front yard for the White House, more or less the size it is today. The area north of the fence, where the Pierce apple trees grew, for a while was called the common, a public green like those found in many American towns and villages. Everything else in the President's Park that could be fenced out was left open for grazing, the cow- and sheep-herders being charged by the day for using it.

Inside his enclosed yard, Jefferson made various improvements, notably in the planting of hundreds of seedling trees, presumably gathered from forests in the region. The glory of the White House grounds would one day be its trees, and although none of Jefferson's is known to survive, he started the tradition. It is an optimistic person who plants a tree. To walk among the groves of the White House today is to recall Jefferson's expression of faith and hope, planting trees whose shade he would not be there to enjoy.

Oak, sycamore, poplar, and cedar joined chestnut, linden, and hickory, all set out in their infancy and protected by wooden boxes. Jefferson formed many of his trees in double lines, allées that framed the house and recalled the radial avenues L'Enfant had planned for the north. From the start, these trees were to have a hard time. Grazing sheep and goats nibbled

Among Jefferson's hobbies was cultivating potted plants in the south windows of his White House office during the winter. His favorite was the geranium. This scarlet variety, published by Robert Sweet in London in 1826, dates from Jefferson's era.

The atlas cedar on the southwest lawn (top), planted before 1900, has grown to great size and once held Amy Carter's tree house. On the southeast a scarlet oak (above) is in full summer leaf. Along the West Colonnade designed by Jefferson (opposite), plants such as leggy hollyhocks now bloom in the summer.

at them; British invaders trampled them; and flames from the White House and the department offices scorched them in 1814, when, at about ten years of age, they should have begun to grow fast, leaf out, and spread.

Jefferson ordered all the major streets of the city lined with Lombardy poplar trees, which grew fast and made a wonderful show of order and stateliness, befitting a capital. Pennsylvania Avenue was supplied with double rows, shading the pedestrian ways that flanked the broad streets. Where the avenue stopped at the White House grounds, on the southeast, Jefferson built an arch of triumph in brick and stone to give formal access to the President's enclave.

On each side of his formidable gate Jefferson planted a weeping willow. These eventually grew very large, spreading out from massive trunks like giant umbrellas drooping with green fringe. It was often said that Presidents entered rejoicing on the north and departed on the south weeping with the willows. Jefferson's plan called for rhododendrons from the mountains, to be planted en masse to screen the south yard from the gate. A curving gravel driveway, beginning at the gate, wound its way to the side of the house and climbed to the public driveway on the north. Jefferson located a flower garden on the east, in the curve of the driveway, but it was not to be planted until fifteen or twenty years later.

Jefferson left his imprint on the grounds. The idea of planting groves of trees was his; he located the flower garden; fences and walls were eventually built where he specified. In defining the purposes of the grounds, he split the property two ways. The north became the public side, for callers scheduled to see the President. Here also curious tourists appeared every day, without appointments. Jefferson ordered these admitted without limit to the state rooms, beginning in the spring of 1801, and except in wartime the White House has been open to the public ever since. The South Grounds were generally considered private and remained inaccessible to the public for many years, until later Presidents chose to open them for concerts and promenades. Passing years saw variations on Jefferson's ideas, but his concept for the garden remained unchanged until well after the Civil War.

The landscape that George Washington envisioned became more yard than park, just as his stone mansion became more house than palace. Except for an extension to the south sixty years later, the size of the White House grounds within the President's Park remains about the same as when Thomas Jefferson fenced them off at the beginning of the nineteenth century.

The Jefferson (or Pierce?) Mounds

The earliest known view of the mounds is this watercolor of the South Lawn, painted just before the Civil War. The mounds provide both privacy and variety in the long sprawl of space. An 1870s schematic drawing proposed yet two more mounds.

The White House is probably the most fully documented house in the United States. Meticulous records— letters, invoices, documentary photographs, and drawings—have been kept since John Adams arrived in 1800; because household accounts are subject to public scrutiny, supporting papers are carefully filed and later permanently stored in the National Archives in Washington.

One garden mystery, however, has not yet been put to rest by these records. It lies in the two abrupt, grassy hillocks on the South Lawn known as the Jefferson Mounds. The accompanying watercolor, made just before the Civil War, shows the western mound.

Just when these mounds were named is not known, but according to oral tradition the dirt was heaped up on orders from Thomas Jefferson sometime between 1801 and 1809. No mention is made of mounds in Jefferson's papers or those of the White House architect Benjamin Henry Latrobe. They do not appear

in graphics before 1860 or so.

Research in manuscripts at the National Archives, however, has yielded a July 12, 1855, letter from the commissioner of public buildings that relates the following: "Earth from excavation for Extension of the Treasury Building was deposited in mounds on the grounds south of the President's House to give an imposing effect to the present flat surface of the lawn." This was forty-six years after Jefferson left office.

Among horticulturalists who had long believed that the mounds were Jefferson's, this discovery brought disbelief—a tradition cast out. Opposition formed.

An elm tree planted by John Quincy Adams between 1825 and 1829 grew near the peak of the eastern mound. When the ancient, gnarled elm died and was cut down in 1991, care was taken to count the growth rings of the severed trunk to determine its age. One hundred fifty-nine rings proved the tree to be as old as John Quincy Adams's time.

How could the mounds have been built in 1855, when so old a tree grew from the upper part of one of them?

"Transplanted," was the historians' response to the horticulturists.

So science challenges the written page; undeniable truth challenges undeniable truth. Members of the resulting two schools of thought on the Jefferson Mounds— each holding to its proof— have not made peace. The hillocks are still called the Jefferson Mounds.

A fter the close of Jefferson's presidency in 1809, no serious gardening took place here for a decade. America entered a war with England. The British marched on Washington in August 1814 and burned the White House, leaving a smoke-blackened stone shell. But within mere months American mortification vanished with victory in New Orleans. The "Second War of Independence" had been won. An amazing two-year building program, conducted by the original architect, James Hoban, brought the White House back, ready for occupancy.

President James Monroe opened his doors to several thousand well-wishers on New Year's Day 1818. Their fear and uncertainty cast aside, the American people enjoyed a sunny confidence. An economic boom was on. To describe his administration, the President adopted the slogan The Era of Good Feelings. He believed that political parties were dead and that the nation would live as one: the dream of the Founders had been realized. Picking up more or less where George Washington had left off, Monroe spent freely making the White House the symbol of his glorious era. Before good feelings soured, considerable was accomplished.

At his New York foundry in 1818 Paulus Hedl made "2 double and 2 single" wrought-iron gates for the north side, mounting them himself by pintels to sandstone gateposts built by stonemasons at work on the Capitol. When the gate hanging was done, the blacksmith presented the President with four keys. The northwest set of Hedl's gates remained in use until 1976, when an attempted forced entry damaged them and President Gerald R. Ford ordered the historic gates stored and replaced with copies in steel.

In the spring of 1818 Monroe purchased from Charles Bulfinch, architect of the Capitol, plans (costing $25 and now lost) for grading and ornamenting the grounds within the fence. To fill the position of White House gardener, Monroe appointed Charles Bizet, who had worked for James and Dolley Payne Madison at their Virginia home, Montpelier. Bizet is usually considered the first gardener of the White House. Jefferson, however, refers in an 1805 letter to a man named

Planting Begins in Earnest

Every June the venerable Jackson magnolia, seen through the stone columns of the South Portico at the peak of its annual performance, renews its ascendancy over the younger botanical population of the grounds, spangling itself with hundreds of cream-colored blossoms and sweetly scenting the air.

Holt, a White House gardener who was pruning trees. Holt thus technically would have been the first gardener.

When Bizet began work, he brought with him an assistant, Thomas McGrath, who supervised the building, after Jefferson's plan, of a stone wall on the north. A year into the construction, "37 gallons and 3 pints of whiskey" were ordered "for the workmen." It was a regular inducement to hurry along. The President had his stone wall by the fall of 1823, when the first frost terminated all building projects requiring mortar.

The full extent of Bizet's gardening is not known, but it seems to have involved mostly preparation of the soil. He graded the grounds, buying dirt by the cart and wagonload from the country and vacant lots in town. Clay reclaimed from the brickmaking operation in 1815–18, when the house was reconstructed, was dumped as fill into the gullies. One low spot, where the White House swimming pool is today, received refuse left from the 1814 fire. The grade continued to rise slowly, load by load, as late as the 1890s. Bizet's other effort was

George Munger painted the burned White House (below) in the fall of 1814. Anne-Marguerite Hyde de Neuville's view of the East Grounds (bottom), about six years later, shows the rebuilt State Department and thick plantings of ornamental trees, some perhaps Jefferson's.

to plant shade trees and fence them in protective boxes painted white.

About 1822 a public square was created on the north and Pennsylvania Avenue was extended between it and the front fence of the house. This was a monumental task, and the change to many seemed radical. One old-timer of the region, while watching the work, poked about the site of the Pierce family's old home and sadly noticed that their tombstones had been piled off to the side to make way for progress. In a sentimental moment he scooped up a handful of dirt from the graveyard and carried it to a Georgetown cemetery, where he scattered it in symbolic memory of those who had once grown tobacco and kept orchards on the land north of the White House.

General Lafayette, visiting America as the nation's guest in 1824 and 1825, was much in evidence at the White House under first Monroe and then John Quincy Adams. His north room overlooked the improvements where the common had

By 1831, when this idyllic south view was published, the White House could be considered completed. Both porticoes were built, and the garden was planted. Artistic license placed the parterre on the west, when in fact it was on the east, where Jefferson had specified.

been. In his honor the newly graded area was named Lafayette Square, today's Lafayette Park.

John Quincy Adams, who followed Monroe in office in 1825, was an experienced gardener who found pleasure and recreation in digging in the dirt himself. Bizet was replaced on August 1, 1825, by John Ousley, whose qualifications—of which we know nothing—seem to have better pleased the President. Quarters were made for Ousley and his family first in the East Wing of the White House and then in a worker's wooden cottage that survived the reconstruction. He remained presidential gardener for nearly thirty years. With Ousley and his enthusiastic patron, gardening at the White House began in earnest.

On days when the weather was fair, Adams took early morning swims in the Potomac, stark naked, attended only by his valet, Antoine Guista, who kept a safety vigil in a rowboat. When he had tired himself sufficiently to guarantee health and longevity, the sixth President dressed on the riverbank and returned to work the soil on his knees beside Ousley. His interest was in plants, not in landscape design. On his travels and walks he picked up seeds and dug small plants to bring back to the White House.

Adams was the first to plant the flower garden that Jefferson had located in his plans southeast of the house. Here he built cold frames to protect tender seedlings and laid out walks, presumably in accord with Bulfinch's master plan. By the summer of 1827 he celebrated his work, which he could see before him from the south window of his upstairs office. He wrote: "In this small garden of not less than two acres there are forest and fruit-trees, shrubs, hedges, esculent vegetables, kitchen and medicinal herbs, hot-house plants, flowers and weeds to the amount, I conjecture, of at least one thousand."

Andrew Jackson, his arch political rival, succeeded Adams in 1829. Ousley stayed on, alone avoiding Jackson's wrath toward those who had served his predecessor. Jackson's wife, Rachel Donelson Jackson, who died between his election and move to Washington, was a flower gardener; Jackson had buried her in her garden at their home in Tennessee. At the White House he gave his support and interest to gardening, and the garden flourished. Numerous laborers were hired to help Ousley. The best gardening equipment appeared, from grub hoes to mole traps.

The first view of gardens at the White House, an English

Charles Bizet, James Monroe's gardener, worked mainly to enrich the White House soil (above). Period botanical depictions show types of trees favored for the grounds (opposite, clockwise from left): white elm (F. A. Michaux, 1817), silver maple (Temple and Beard nursery catalogue, 1886), Magnolia grandiflora (F. A. Michaux, The North American Silva, 1819), and Norway maple (Ludwig Pfleger, 1788).

engraving published in 1831, was made while Jackson was President. It has its inaccuracies but gives the flavor, showing curving paths and flower beds, a smooth-rolled lawn, and a general orderliness that early descriptions suggest had not previously been typical of the White House grounds. What had been raw earth covered with debris a mere three decades before was now polished considerably.

Seeds for Jackson were ordered from the Flushing, New York, companies of William Prince and Sons and Bloodgood and Company, which were among the nation's earliest large-scale nurseries. Elm trees, purchased to line the streets of the city, were also planted on the White House grounds. Silver and sugar maples, red-twigged lindens, oaks, European and American sycamores, and the white-blossomed horse chestnut were set out not in allées or formal lines but more as trees seeded in nature—scattered apparently without plan, to achieve a picturesque effect.

The garden's paths were graveled and raked to mounds in the center, then rolled smooth with a heavy stone roller. Framed by grass borders, the walks led among flower beds carefully groomed and planted with flowering plants of many species, including foxglove, dragonhead, sweet William, and daisies. Other plantings doubtlessly included common garden varieties that were not bought but propagated in neighboring gardens and given or traded in the age-old way among gardeners, a practice still followed at the White House.

Flowers that were not in beds included roses trained on "Espalier Frames" and annuals planted in lime-washed, terra-cotta pots. A long wooden arbor painted white sheltered a walk along the west side of the garden. Today's show of spring bulbs at the White House has its ancestry in Jackson's garden, where tulips, hyacinths, and iris bloomed for "Old Hickory." But this was only one feature of Jackson's gardening program.

Ralph E. W. Earl's portrait of Andrew Jackson (above), painted in 1834, shows Jefferson's arch of triumph and willow trees. In 1818 the blacksmith Paulus Hedl provided several options for a wrought-iron railing for the north side of the house (right); the lower one was built and remained until 1902. Tulips still bloom in the spring in the Rose Garden (opposite).

At the north end of the garden in Andrew Jackson's administration stood a rectangular brick shell of a building, a relic of Jefferson's failed plan to connect the White House to the flanking office buildings. This long thick-walled structure of one story had been built by Benjamin Henry Latrobe as a fireproof archives for the Treasury. Although it survived the British torches in 1814, it was left ruined, and its colonnade, intended to link with the East Colonnade, was never built.

The Orangery

The building was closed in roughly as a stable where certain Treasury and State Department employees kept their official horses. John Ousley, the White House gardener, also used part of it to store his tools and supplies. In 1835 Andrew Jackson turned the ruin into an orangery for the White House, permitting the indoor cultivation year-round of citrus fruits to serve the dinner table and medicine chest.

The orangery, or hothouse, was so successful that gardening under glass remained part of White House life for the balance of the century. As remodeled, the orangery provided a row of simple rooms with half-moon transom windows on the north, where the building backed into the slope and left only the upper third of the wall exposed; full glass windows on the opposite wall drank in the southern sun, which the heavy masonry walls contained through most of the cold nights. Whitewashed inside to further reflect the natural light, this plant house was considered an orangery, not a greenhouse, only because it had no overhead glass.

The idea was neither new nor unique. George Washington had built a smaller orangery at Mount Vernon. Andrew Jackson had seen it, still in operation. When it burned to its brick walls in the bitter winter of 1835, the Washington heirs presented President Jackson with a rescued Malayan sago, or feather, palm that had been grown there from seeds by the Father of His Country. This palm not only went to safe harbor in the new White House orangery; its preservation may also have been the reason Jackson ordered the orangery built, for he collected Washington relics.

The most common way to garden under glass was to use a

The formerly open passage between the West Colonnade and the house is glazed and used today much as the orangery was when it flourished from 1835 until 1857 and contained fruit trees and camellias. Here a clipped bay laurel and other greenery drink in the winter sun.

glass jar or bowl or a domed bell jar (a *cloche*) made for the purpose. Placed over tender plants, these ensured warmth from late winter to spring. Any American home with yard space was likely to have a plant pit—more a greenhouse than an orangery—with a slanted roof of ordinary window sash topping a dugout cellar with walls usually of brick or sometimes wood. Here the growing season could begin earlier in pots than was possible outside in the ground, and delicate plants such as fruit trees could be wintered over before being brought out for warm weather.

More complicated hothouses, like those at the White House and Mount Vernon, had heating systems of some sort. Such an arrangement typically featured a fireplace with flues to move hot air and smoke beneath the brick floor. The White House orangery had a stove to thwart damage on extremely cold and overcast days, but the significant heat came from winter sun, which made the orangery's interior, with its thick crowd of plants, a tropical Eden. In warm weather, the potted contents of the orangery were set about outside on the garden walks or, in the case of the more delicate fruit trees, along the north driveway, away from the direct summer sun.

The interest in orangeries at the White House in the 1830s accompanied improved means of transporting plants worldwide. Shipped for centuries by land and sea, plants had always been difficult to relocate. Most of the roses that poured from China to the West for hundreds of years probably came as seeds. The development in England in the late 1830s of the Wardian case, a portable hothouse with glass sides and top, allowed the movement of cold-wary seedlings as well as mature plants. Selling plants internationally became commercially feasible, and for the President more interesting plant material now came by Potomac steamer and rail.

Potted fruit trees in the White House orangery soon gained the company of tubbed ornamental camellias; likely to be nipped outside sooner or later in Washington's erratic climate, in the orangery they bloomed most of the year, rich in blossoms and dark, glossy leaves. Jessie Benton Frémont, daughter of the celebrated Sen. Thomas Hart Benton from Missouri and wife of the "Pathfinder," John C. Frémont, recalled that in the 1830s White House camellias were brought inside for parties, lined "row upon row," making a garden indoors. The red, pink, or white blossoms produced by these plants were small, not much bigger than a silver dollar and commonly called japonicas.

Documents of the 1830s and 1840s suggest the wide variety of indoor plants that would appear at the White House in the

In 1853 Franklin Pierce ordered several varieties of camellia for the orangery, including the 'Variegata' shown in a hand-colored engraving from 1843 (Lorenzo Berlèse, Iconographie du genre camellia, *1843).*

last half of the century. Other than fruit trees, camellias and roses were the primary tenants of the orangery's stepped tables. There seems to have been little else. Vines such as Carolina jessamine and climbing wisteria appear in descriptions, but they are not noted in plant orders for the orangery, nor are geraniums, which were seen often at the White House then.

The garden and orangery were lovingly cared for after Jackson left. His immediate successor, Martin Van Buren (1837–41), had a taste for gardening and while American minister to Great Britain had made a tour of English gardens with the author Washington Irving. As President, he encouraged Ousley's work—perhaps too much—for soon enough the garden became a political issue. Congressman Charles Ogle of Pennsylvania looked into the public disbursement records and was shocked by the amount of money the President spent on the "palace."

With feigned outrage, Ogle delivered his giddy oration to Congress in the spring of 1840. It being a presidential election year, in the midst of a depression, the speech was widely published. When Ogle was through, Van Buren had been painted as extravagant and superficial; by contrast his Whig opponent in the heated race, the military hero William Henry Harrison, was the picture of log-cabin simplicity. Ogle broadcast Van Buren's indulgences in personal luxury as being enjoyed entirely at public expense. He ate from gold spoons, washing his "pretty tapering, soft, white lily fingers" in "Fanny Kemble green finger cups."

The President had built a garden at the White House that rivaled Versailles. By merely interpreting the bills on record, Ogle described presidential extravagance in "building dwarf walls and coping, constructing fountains, paving footways, planting, transplanting, pruning and dressing horse chestnuts, lindens, beds and borders, training and irrigating honey suckles, trumpet creepers, primroses, lady slippers, and dandelions, cultivating sweet-scented grass, and preparing beautiful bouquets for the palace saloons."

But for all of Ogle's embellishments, in the era of the "common man" his harshest accusation was true: "As the President's garden is enclosed by a high stone wall, and as the gates are generally secured with locks, very few persons, I have been informed, visit it, except by special invitation. . . . I have been in the garden twice; but on both occasions, we (another member was in company) were compelled, on reaching the western end of this garden, to clamber over the stone wall, finding the gates locked."

During the 1850s greenhouses with overhead glass generally

This 1858 photograph documenting construction of the Treasury Department is the only known photograph of the old garden and orangery of the White House, here merely details in the larger photograph. The orangery is on the right, a long arbor on the left.

replaced orangeries, and the White House orangery was remodeled with glass shed roofs to the south in 1853. President Franklin Pierce (1853–57) took an interest in the greenhouse and built a semioctagonal bay in the middle of the long range of glass sheds for a sitting room. The new south facade was largely of glass. Twelve back-painted glass panels tinted the sunlight that fell inside: claret, yellow, green, and blue, coloring the white plaster walls, cast-iron furniture, and surrounding banks of palms. Large pots held yucca and trailing vines. Running water in India rubber hoses kept the leaves wet and the tile floor gleaming. Through French doors company gathered inside looked out on a mown and rolled lawn, incised with flower beds, crossed by graveled walks, and framed by trees.

An order for plant material in the fall of 1853, when the greenhouse extension was completed, shows that the camellia remained the favorite flower. Camellias ordered at that time included "The Queen of Whites, Lady Anne's Blush, Duchess d'Orleans, Palmer's Perfection, Miss Percival, Douglass White, Variegata." Every spring large orders were placed for such plant material to be sent to Washington by rail.

To the remodeled greenhouse in 1855 were brought the botanical specimens from China and Japan collected by Commodore Matthew C. Perry. Congress had already appropriated funds to build a national greenhouse (the current National Botanic Garden). The President's effort to channel these funds to an expansion of the White House orangery was thwarted without hesitation by Congress, but for two years the shelves of the building and the walks of the garden were crowded with potted specimens from Japan. Perry, himself a botanist, accompanied Pierce among the pots and tubs, explaining the significance of each plant and how he had obtained it.

Just before he left office Pierce was forced to authorize the demolition of the orangery and garden to make way for an extension of the Treasury Department on the east. Some of the White House grounds had to be sacrificed to accommodate the new wing and a street to be laid between the two. The garden originally located in Jefferson's plan would go, to be replaced by the large, columned south facade of the Treasury that still stands.

President Pierce wanted a substitute for the orangery and garden that would approximate their domestic pleasures. The solution was to build a new greenhouse atop the flat roof of the West Colonnade, to be entered from the end of the house. This conservatory would bring blossoms and fragrance up close. Flowers would now mean more at the White House than they ever had before.

White House gardeners have grown oranges in pots since Jefferson's time, including this edible China orange (below), published by Antoine Risso and Antoine Poiteau of Paris in 1818. A hardy orange, an ornamental tree with inedible fruit, shades the White House on the South Grounds (opposite).

GARDENING IN

DOORS AND OUT

F lowers became permanently established in White House life beginning in Andrew Jackson's era, with potted plants in bloom grown under glass. The use of cut flowers in vases did not appear until the late 1850s, when James Buchanan's niece and hostess, Harriet Lane, importing the taste from England, anticipated and hastened an enduring White House affection for flower arrangements.

Mrs. Clement C. Clay Jr., a senator's wife and frequent visitor to the White House in the Buchanan period (1857–61), remembered the "remarkable bouquets" enjoyed at the White House on the eve of the Civil War. "They were stiff and formal things," she wrote, "as big round as a breakfast plate, and invariably composed of a half-dozen wired japonicas [camellias] ornamented with a pretentious cape of marvellously wrought lace-paper. At every plate, at every State dinner, lay one of these rigid bouquets. This fashion, originating at the White House, was taken up by all Washington. For an entire season the japonica was the only flower seen at the houses of the fashionable or mixing in the toilettes of the belles."

Only wax flowers had previously been seen either on White House dinner tables or in the parlors. James Monroe's French porcelain vases, which are still in use, always held wax flowers in his time (1817–24) and for twenty years afterward; they were displayed under glass domes to protect them from dust and destruction by the fireplace heat. Fine old wax flowers shared that delicate, ethereal, even eerie realism of a doll's face. Sometimes white, sometimes tinted natural colors, they were usually imported from France, but in the first decades of the nineteenth century they were available from the French and Belgian émigré communities in New York and Philadelphia. Making wax flowers was a recognized decorative art.

The bouquets and boutonnières of real flowers that dinner guests found as favors at their places preceded the use of cut flowers in vases. Although documentation for flowers as decoration is scant and vague even when found, camellias and roses are the earliest fresh flowers mentioned in White House records. By the late 1860s, especially with the advent to the presidency of Ulysses S. Grant (1869–77), the White House abounded in flowers. Julia Dent Grant was likely to turn the

Flowers Under Glass

The West Colonnade built by Jefferson (preceding pages) stands as repaired after the War of 1812 and frames two sides of the Rose Garden. Here it rises above waves of fall chrysanthemums and blue 'Victoria' salvia. Amaryllis, forced in pots (opposite), bloom in the current residence greenhouse, a small room tucked away behind the roof's stone balustrade.

dinner table into a bower of roses or lilacs. She honored her successor, Lucy Webb Hayes, at tea by seating her beneath a canopy of pink azaleas. When Mrs. Grant left the White House, she said, not without regret, that she was leaving a beautiful world of orchids.

As an agrarian world slowly began to turn urban with industrialization, pastoral memories helped inspire in city people a wish to cultivate flowers. If not a return to the soil in fact, this symbolic resurrection of old ways recognized a long and nearly universal heritage of making things grow. Floriculture for both public and private gardens had become important in Europe as well. The appearances of new varieties of lilies and fragrant flowers were greeted with the enthusiasm shown today for recordings and best sellers. Gardening became to Americans a democratic expression that cut across class lines. Flowers grew in tin cans and costly conservatories alike—the flowers themselves showing no preference—and planting inside was a hobby with city folk, who had no place to garden outside.

The love of flowers led to an increased use of what Europeans called winter gardens. Whether in a simple bay window added to a house or in separate buildings, greenhouse gardening gained an important presence in the American home. The White House was no exception, beginning with the orangery, created in 1835, and moving adjacent to the house itself in 1857. From this latter structure, the White House conservatories grew and grew over forty-five years, climaxing at the century's end in a rambling Taj Mahal of glass.

Cultivating masses of indoor plants became a national pastime between the Civil War and World War I. Greenhouses, built first to supply fruits out of season, by the 1860s had another practical function: as appendages to the house, they introduced welcomed humidity to the dry, stifling air of gravity-flow, hot-air central heating. To heat some of the rooms of the White House, such a system had been installed in 1837 by Van Buren. Franklin Pierce (1853–57)

When Ulysses S. Grant ordered his presidential china for the White House, he specified flowers. On this soup plate a wild rose is encircled with a buff band and crowned with the American eagle.

might have moved the greenhouse anywhere on the grounds. Locating it on the west terrace was a move influenced by the desperate need for humidity in the house.

The White House greenhouse of 1857, completed during Buchanan's term, was apparently even simpler than the early orangery, which before Pierce's improvements served more as a working greenhouse than a tropical sitting room or retreat. The new wooden structure had a glass ceiling and sides and salvaged the stained-glass panels from the orangery. The same stepped shelves, the same wooden tables, the same thick-rimmed terra-cotta pots, planted with fruit trees, roses, camellias, and some palms, determined the structure's character. George Washington's sago palm from Mount Vernon was elevated importantly in the center.

This was the greenhouse through which Harriet Lane and her friends walked with Britain's young Prince of Wales in 1860, while the Marine Band played "Listen to the Mockingbird." A news reporter was allowed a look inside: "As you enter the conservatory itself it seems almost like penetrating the luxurious fragrance of some South American island, so warm and odiferous is the atmosphere.... Here you may see orange trees, and a lemon tree ... rows of prickly cactus of every size and shape ... camellia japonica, delicate spirea, ardisia, and poinsettia."

At times during the 1850s the White House grounds were open to promenaders. This picturesque engraving depicts the South Grounds during James Buchanan's administration, just before the Civil War. The new greenhouse from 1857 is shown atop the West Colonnade.

Two eras under glass: the greenhouse of 1857 (above) being shown to visiting Plains Indians about 1862 by Abraham Lincoln's secretary, George Nicolay, center rear; and the greenhouse in 1877 (opposite), in which Lucy Webb Hayes, son Scott, daughter Fannie, standing, and a friend pose.

This was also the greenhouse of Lincoln's day, where the family found privacy during the Civil War; the same greenhouse that gave John Watt, the chief gardener, access to a lonely Mary Todd Lincoln, who would be drawn under the glare of suspicion herself when Watt was accused of spying on the White House for the Confederate underground. Among blooming azaleas and camellias, the Lincolns had a distracting place close at hand to escape from the exhausting demands of politics and the war, but in fact the President seems to have taken little interest in it.

The structure burned in the winter of 1867, with a great loss of plants, including the Washington palm. It was replaced by a larger greenhouse of iron frame and wood sash, designed by Alfred B. Mullett, supervising architect of the Treasury. An invoice from Robert Buist Jr. dated the summer of 1867 shows an order for "Liliums, oxalis, Tube Roses, Gladiolus, Hyacinths," perhaps to be forced in pots in the greenhouse during the coming winter. President Grant expanded the greenhouse. He took great delight in flowers, and it seemed perfectly natural to him to build a billiard room with china spittoons between the greenhouse and the mansion.

Any change at the White House is destined to have a political side, and the greenhouse was no exception. Julia Grant took advantage of the hothouse floral bounty to revise the old and tedious custom of social calling, begun by the effervescent Dolley Madison in 1809. It was a friendly and flattering gesture from the President's wife to newcomers and visitors in a small-town capital. But through the years calling had grown into an ordeal to be faced every week. The First Lady had to be driven about in the President's coach, dressed elegantly in hat, veil, gloves, and hot, high-necked, long-sleeved silk dress, to make fifteen-minute calls on important women visiting the city and the wives of new congressmen and senators.

The gracious custom, naturally laced with political implication, sparked the most vicious gossip, rivalry, and jealousy and became so delicate that the prospect of it frightened new First Ladies. None was willing to end the custom since Elizabeth Kortright Monroe in 1818 had embarrassed her husband in the attempt. Fifty years later, faced with eight or ten calls in a morning, three days a week, to homes, boardinghouses, and hotels, Mrs. Grant took a fresh look.

A shrewd woman in situations of this kind, she decided to send bouquets instead. She had them made from greenhouse and garden flowers and sent out along with an engraved card, via liveried footman, in the White House coach. At the appropriate places the footman went to the door or lobby and with a sweeping bow and a click of the heels left the pretty gift.

The bouquets, ready to be inserted into a vase at home, varied from roses to orchids to hydrangeas, interspersed with palm fronds and ferns, framed in frilly paper doilies of gold

A view of the North Grounds about 1895 (below left) shows the "French gurg" steam-driven fountain, which had been installed in 1871. The roof of the West Colonnade, with the conservatories removed (below right), became a romantic promenade after Theodore Roosevelt's remodeling of 1902.

or white. Each bouquet was wrapped in tissue paper and handsomely boxed. Now and then these paper relics, with their White House initials and the little card noting "Compliments of Mrs. Grant, the Executive Mansion," are found folded away, cherished, in old trunks. The White House staff in Julia Grant's day listed a bouquet maker, and by the late 1890s there were three.

The abstemious Rutherford B. Hayes (1877–81) judged Grant's billiard room next to the greenhouse unrefined. He replaced it with a tile-floored palm court, where he struck up vigorous promenades, offered to guests after dinner in lieu of the traditional liqueurs. By the late 1870s the greenhouse or conservatory, as it came to be called, was a fairyland of plants and flowers. Its many varieties of roses and orchids were notable.

Hayes started the custom of decorating the grounds in the summer with plants from the conservatory. Under the gardener he brought from Cincinnati, Henry Pfister, choice greenhouse plants in great number were arranged on the North Lawn, between the two arms of the driveway. Lines of pots, circles of pots, flowering things, palms—the White House gave a hot-weather show that the city and visitors came to anticipate with delight.

Sometimes in the summer, parterres were cut into the carpet of lawn on the north much like today's Flower Library maintained by the National Park Service on the Tidal Basin opposite the Jefferson Memorial. From paisleys and daisies to circles and serpentine beds, the forms varied, but the effect, mixed with the potted plants from the conservatory, was always splendid.

The first Roosevelts' tastes in flower arranging: a select few long-stemmed roses and lilies in tall glass vases in the "international" setting of the redecorated Red Room (below left); and an opulent East Room dinner in 1901 with flowers overflowing the tables (below right).

During most of the Victorian presidencies, the conservatory was in constant use by the residents of the White House. Children played there when the weather was bad. More than one coddled pony munched greenery along the paths. The family was able to take its walks there in private. Grover Cleveland (1885–89, 1893–97), considered a rough, blustery sort of man, was nevertheless pleased to bend over and sniff his favorite flowers when he believed that he was unseen; betrayed in the act by the walls of glass, through which a fascinated household staff watched, he soon lost all pretense of hiding his gentle interest. He and his sisters ordered a lavish display of conservatory flowers and plants to decorate his celebrated Blue Room wedding on June 2, 1886.

Cleveland's young and beautiful wife, Frances Folsom Cleveland, loved orchids, so the conservatory began to brim with them. Sometimes, when one of the adoring White House staff saw her linger over a particular flower, a message was relayed upstairs to Octavius Prudom, a presidential clerk with an artistic flair. He hurried to the scene when she left and painted a watercolor, and that evening at bedtime a chamber maid slipped the picture and the original flower on Frankie Cleveland's pillow.

When Theodore Roosevelt began his major remodeling of the White House in 1902, the conservatory covered half again as much space as any floor of the house. The glass houses rambled atop the West Colonnade and out over the old stable, showing roofs slanted, pointed, and curved. Jefferson's porches, completely encapsulated in the complex, looked out into a rose garden under glass, misting fountain in the center, and year-round bloom. There was a fern house, an orchid house, palm rooms, the roses and camellias everywhere in large number. Walkways of wooden slats sometimes softened by cocoa matting passed between the rows of pots and copper-lined planting beds. Plumbing pipes overhead provided rainlike watering. On a winter day one could look out into the falling snow from a spring garden inside.

In carrying out Roosevelt's changes in 1902, the architect Charles McKim insisted that the "old colonial" character of the White House could never be restored to its George Washington purity with the glass houses intact. The President reluctantly supposed that this was so. Edith Carow Roosevelt hesitated but under pressure conceded, on the condition that the conservatory be rebuilt at another location. The remodeling was done in haste. Henry Pfister, the gardener for nearly thirty years, saw his plants cast out. Most of them were lost in an early frost.

The White House conservatories had their heyday about 1895 (opposite top). Two interiors, or "houses," at about the same time show one filled primarily with camellias (bottom left) and the other lush with chrysanthemums, lilies, and palms (bottom right).

The
Greenhouse
Today

Clipped myrtle trees in tubs (above right) await transport from the greenhouse to a White House function. Cuttings on shelves (opposite, clockwise from top left) include cyclamen, variegated hydrangea, fuchsia for topiaries, and pink 'Wendy Anne' geraniums.

Greenhouses are now little more than a memory at the White House, and the relatively few flowers grow mainly outside, near the house. Blossoms are secondary to the lawns, shrubbery, and vines as features for seasonal color in a larger, naturalistic setting of trees. But living plants and flowers remain part of the tradition of White House hospitality. They give the house warmth and color and say, symbolically and otherwise, that an effort was made to have things looking good for all who go there to enjoy the President's hospitality.

The White House conservatory was replaced in 1903 by a relatively simple greenhouse located at the present site of the Smithsonian Institution's National Museum of American History on the Mall. Although that greenhouse is long gone, White House greenhouses still exist off site. The present one is near the Aquatic Garden in

the city's Kenilworth section.

From there palms, tubbed laurels, ferns, and other greenery are taken as needed for the White House. To the greenhouse potted plants, from trees to simple chrysanthemums, are brought for "rest and relaxation" under the glass roofs, where they receive expert care. Delivery trucks move greenhouse material to and from the White House. Does the First Lady need a background of blooming orange trees for her awards ceremony? They are readily available from the greenhouse. Two pots of gardenia bushes in bloom? Given a little notice, existing plants can be forced into flower and brought to the house as required.

If the particular request cannot be satisfied without borrowing from another nursery, alternatives exist. Magnificent flowers and fruit trees bloom nearly all year beneath the glass, a tradition dating to Andrew Jackson's presidency. A few orchids are available, although the extent of orchid raising generally depends on the interest of the President or his wife and has never approximated what it was before 1902, in the days of the old conservatory. Roses are there in some abundance— miniatures to be potted in antique porcelain vases— along with clipped trees, of which laurel, planted in tubs, is an enduring favorite. ✣

Flower Arranging

The thirteen-foot-long, gilt-bronze plateau purchased for James Monroe in Paris in 1817 might claim to be the oldest "vase" for flower arranging at the White House. Assembled in its entirety, it is arranged in the Victorian manner with warm, contemporary colors of 'Osiana', 'Rodeo', and 'Cream Essence' roses, delphinium, lavender statice, maidenhair fern, and swags of smilax.

Flower arranging has been a constant at the White House for more than a century. Stands of camellias, probably tubbed and on pedestals, adorned some of Andrew Jackson's receptions in the 1830s, but cut flowers did not decorate dinner tables or fill parlor vases until the late 1850s, under James Buchanan's youthful niece and hostess, Harriet Lane.

According to the budget and what the President's wife wishes, flowers are available for every occasion and every space in the White House. For most of this century, this has meant formal mass displays or tailored arrangements, usually domes of roses and spring flowers, placed close together. Jacqueline Bouvier Kennedy generally banned roses in favor of tulips, daisies, and bright garden flowers.

In 1981 Nancy Davis Reagan introduced more colors and more muted hues. Her successor in 1989, Barbara Pierce Bush, a horticulturist, expanded this more modern mode with subtle color mixtures. In the skilled hands of the White House florist Nancy Clarke, flower arranging entered a creative orbit all its own. Hillary Rodham Clinton encouraged and extended this change with elegant arrangements for state occasions. Floral masterpieces now vary from formal sprays of roses to amaryllis bound in straw or sunflowers mixed with ivy.

Occupants of the White House have always been interested in flowers. The widower Jefferson's office windows were crowded with geraniums, but floral arrangements were largely features of formal occasions and were not everyday fare until the twentieth century. The art of cut flower arranging came with Julia Grant in the 1870s. She adorned the dining room table with flowers of all kinds that

were fixed into garlands, arches, and sprays. In 1876 she banished the famous James Monroe plateau pictured here in favor of a silver centerpiece showing Hiawatha rowing his canoe, arranged with orchids and ferns supplied by the conservatory.

The Victorian attraction for spare Japanese flower arranging appeared at the White House with the bouquet makers, also in the early 1870s. While these forms remained, they were never as popular as large, loose arrangements, because the rooms are sizable, with high ceilings, and tend to dwarf smaller floral creations.

In the remodeled White House of 1902, Edith Roosevelt mixed French statuettes of dancers among the flower arrangements on the dining room table. She liked flowers that appeared arranged as an afterthought, as though plucked from her colonial garden and simply put in a vase. The bouquet makers departed during the Roosevelt Administration, but Mrs. Roosevelt had an eager accomplice in Henry Pfister, the gardener who had lost his conservatory, and they kept the White House more consistently decorated with vases of flowers than it had ever been before. Her favorite centerpieces were full-blown roses, in pinks and yellows, and this choice of flowers pleased her successors for more than fifty years. ❧

A fter Theodore Roosevelt's remodeling of 1902, flower growing moved outside and was determined by the seasons. There were to be no more camellias in February, nor in fact ever again as many flowers as the White House had produced in the years of the conservatory.

Flowers in the Gardens

A pergola covered with Concord grapes terminates the west end of the East Garden. The hanging baskets contain 'Hekla' chrysanthemums. Bordered by an osmanthus hedge, the flower bed in the foreground features salvia and chrysanthemums in pots.

Edith Roosevelt enjoyed flowers. After the loss of the conservatory she, with the help of the venerable gardener Henry Pfister, designed an intricately patterned "colonial garden." It stood in the open area once occupied by the rose house within the glass confines of the greenhouse beginning in the late 1870s. The new garden brimmed with old-fashioned hollyhocks, phlox, sweet William, black-eyed Susan, sweet peas, cockscomb, all contained within ribbonlike borders of boxwood.

The colonial-style garden was replaced in 1913, when Ellen Axson Wilson, the first wife of Woodrow Wilson (1913–21), planted a rose garden on the site of the current Rose Garden almost immediately after moving to the White House. Mrs. Wilson's garden was the antithesis of the quaint, calico-patterned design Mrs. Roosevelt had planted. The rose garden of 1913 was rigid, formal, and green, with sharp corners and long vistas, in the manner of seventeenth-century Italian gardens.

Ellen Wilson was one of the most dedicated of all White House gardeners. A painter in oils, she had considerable talent as an artist of landscapes and still lifes and brought her aesthetic eye to the garden in determining form and color. Although her rose garden grew specimen roses, the dominant color was green, with high privet hedges and a clipped lawn. She was assisted in her design by the well-known landscape architect George Burnap, who completed the final stages of the garden after her sudden death at the White House on August 6, 1914.

Among the prominent landscape designers that Mrs. Wilson brought to the White House was Beatrix Farrand, later the designer of Washington's noted Dumbarton Oaks garden (1921–47). Farrand made a plan for the garden on the east side, which since 1902 had not been landscaped with anything other than a few rows of sculptural junipers and other architectural evergreens. Farrand's design of 1913, an effort to be faintly Victorian or old-fashioned, is close to the form the garden took and has kept since then. When the East Garden was new, it was planted in spring bulbs and summer and fall flowers. In winter

Among the First Ladies interested in gardening was Edith Carow Roosevelt. When the French nation commissioned her portrait (right) by Theobald Chartran in 1902, both artist and sitter agreed that the setting should be the colonial garden (below), which Mrs. Roosevelt and the White House gardener Henry Pfister had designed.

In 1913 Woodrow Wilson's first wife, Ellen Axson Wilson, replaced the colonial garden with the first rose garden (below). After her death the following August, the East Garden (left) was completed by the landscape designer Beatrix Farrand. President Wilson and his second wife, Edith Bolling Wilson, posed there in 1916.

its permanent outlines of boxwood and ivy borders preserved the sharp-edged, rectangular definition of the plan.

The gardens on the east and west, planted generally as Ellen Wilson had approved, were maintained fairly much in the same form until the Kennedy Administration. Time modified the crispness of the hedges, and specimen roses had dwindled to an assortment of nursery stock. In 1961 John F. Kennedy (1961–63) read a friend's copy of Thomas Jefferson's notes on gardening and became interested in improving the White House gardens.

Among his principal innovations was a redesign of the rose garden on the west to make it double as a place to hold outdoor ceremonies. Adjacent to the Oval Office and embraced on two sides by colonnades, the setting had all the elements for what the President had in mind. He asked Rachel Lambert Mellon to supervise the design, and she turned to the landscape architect Perry Wheeler. Together they produced a plan that was executed by Irvin M. Williams, who at their urging had been appointed superintendent of grounds for the White House.

The Rose Garden now consists of a long, broad lawn flanked by flower beds subdivided by boxwood hedges and lined with saucer magnolia and crab apple trees. At the western end limestone steps provide a platform that can hold a podium. The lawn accommodates one thousand spectators, yet when not in use for presentations it is simply the central green carpet of an intimate flower garden.

Success with the Rose Garden inspired a revision of the garden on the east, a project designed in the Kennedy Administration but completed under Lyndon B. Johnson (1963–69). Dedicated by Lady Bird Taylor Johnson to Jacqueline Kennedy, the East Garden was reconfigured to feature seasonal flowers and ornamental hedges. Here Mrs. Mellon honored Beatrix Farrand's concept of 1913 but added more flower beds and relocated the fish pool to the east, matched by a pergola on the west. Known variously as the Jacqueline Kennedy Garden, the First Ladies' Garden, and the East Garden, this is the garden seen by millions of visitors whose tour of the White House takes them along the East Colonnade for a close look.

Walking to the Oval Office, the President can see the Rose Garden in spring (opposite) and summer (top). Beyond this enclave, behind thick screens of trees and shrubbery, is the "back-yard" swimming pool built for Gerald Ford (above).

67

In the Rose Garden varieties of white and pink lilies (top and above) are staggered to bloom all summer. The garden presents its summer bounty of caladiums, hostas, geraniums, hollyhocks, and dusty miller (opposite), followed by autumn's salvia and chrysanthemums (page 70). Seen in the snow, the Rose Garden proves that a classical garden plan holds its form even in the winter (page 71).

For most of the twentieth century floriculture at the White House has taken place in the East and West Gardens. Because the Washington climate is somewhat northern and somewhat southern, the length of the spring season is hard to predict. The show time for White House flowers is, of course, spring, especially April and May. The White House can depend on at least three weeks of flowers, but now and then it receives six or even eight.

A wet fall and a cold winter generally promise a beautiful spring. It is not wholly odd to see crocuses' color through a blanket of April snow or the first of the pink magnolias nipped by frost. In April, when the Japanese cherry blossoms begin to open along the Tidal Basin, the White House garden awakens in light green leaves, sprawls of emerald lawn, and flowers of all kinds.

White House gardeners use annuals to make the blooming seasons as long as possible. Rings of red tulips and brilliant purplish blue grape hyacinths around the fountains are a tradition of more than thirty years. For summer, the tulip bulbs are dug up and discarded and the beds receive scarlet salvia and canna lilies.

Both the East and West Gardens, being close to the house, are protected from the damaging northwest wind and served by thick stone walls that absorb the heat of the winter sun and hold it well into the night. Delicate flowers subject to damage by late frosts nearly always survive in the protection of these gardens.

The Rose Garden on the west has as its signature tree the 'Katherine' crab apple that blooms, protected here, in May. It makes light pink clouds of flowers over two long side beds containing thousands of tulips, daffodils, hyacinth, and other spring flowers in reds, yellows, blues, and white. In the East Garden, seasonal color, including fruit trees, stands out against the dazzling white of the building, the grass, and the larger sheared hedges.

Flowering trees spill over from the two gardens down onto the groves that flank the South Lawn. June brings out the white spike blossoms of the buckeyes, a horse chestnut planted in honor of the state of Ohio, home of six Presidents. Dogwood, which grows almost like a weed in the Potomac region and must have greeted George Washington and Pierre L'Enfant from the edges of the woods when they came here in 1792, blooms white and also hybrid pink. It seeks shade, so the tree flourishes near other trees. Walks through the trees reveal dogwood and rhododendron en masse, in the same sort of clumps that Jefferson planned for the grounds.

By July the White House landscape has settled into summer. The dusty miller, geraniums, and blue floss flower are introduced

The East Garden (below), seen from the Lincoln Sitting Room upstairs, is in use as an art gallery. Looking back (opposite), the garden has a fall display of chrysanthemum topiaries and American holly, rising from a bed of mums of mixed varieties.

to perennial candytuft, lavender, and such herbs as thyme, rosemary, chives, and mint. Blue water lilies share the Children's Garden with masses of yellow-petaled black-eyed Susans. Old-fashioned flowers bloom close to the house. Pots lined up along the porticoes brim with white petunias and red geraniums.

Primary among the fall flowers are chrysanthemums of many varieties: yellow 'Freedom', white 'Fujii Joanette', orange 'Pumpkin', apricot 'Sandy', and others. Spoon chrysanthemums and violet blue salvia join the existing herbs. By December the color is gone and the gardens are green gardens. Their more or less classical lines, the long beds, and the ninety-degree corners incised into lawn are handsome to see even in the cold months, when rain makes them glisten and darkens the raw dirt to black or snow covers them, revealing in thin outline the forms of beds, trees, and walks.

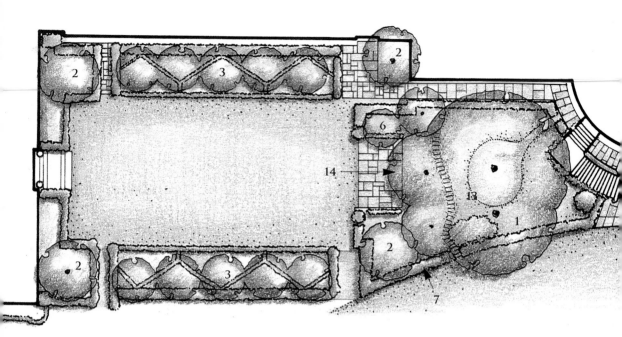

The East and West Gardens

The West Garden (above) has been known as the Rose Garden since 1913, and the East Garden (opposite) is variously called the First Ladies' and the Jacqueline Kennedy Garden.

The East and West (Rose) Gardens are the principal flower gardens of the White House. Both are formal yet are relaxed by parades of seasonal color, their hedge-lined beds becoming baskets of flowers. The two gardens are somewhat similar in design in that they feature a rectangular carpet of grass in the center surrounded by flower beds. Colonnades provide walkways around part of the West Garden perimeter, while open grass paths in the East Garden permit close contact with the planting beds. Following are lists of key plantings and garden ornaments and a sample of seasonal plantings for spring, summer, and fall.

KEY PLANTINGS

1. Jackson Southern magnolias
2. Kennedy saucer magnolias
3. 'Katherine' crab apples
4. Littleleaf lindens
5. American hollies
6. Washington hawthorn
7. Holly osmanthus

GARDEN ORNAMENTS

8. Pergola (1965)
9. Trellis and window (1982)
10. Sculpture (Silvia Shaw Judson, 1965)
11. Pool (1965)
12. Benches (1850)
13. Furniture (gift of Amelia Riggs, 1973)
14. Wooden bench (gift of Rachel Lambert Mellon, 1983)

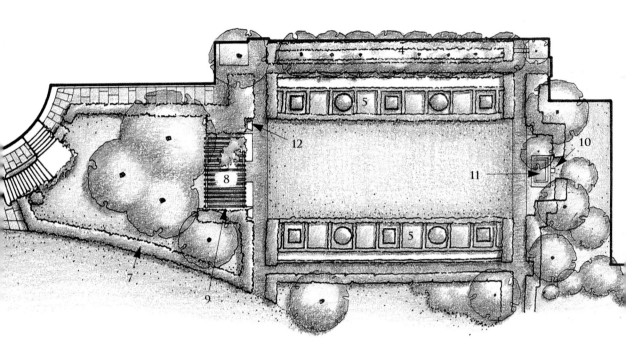

Rose Garden Spring Flowers

'Nancy Reagan' hybrid tea rose
'Pat Nixon' floribunda rose
'White Lightnin'' grandiflora
    rose
'Sea Foam' shrub rose
'Elegans' siebold hosta
'Boutonniere' cottage pinks
'Purissima' and 'Red Emperor'
    Fosteriana tulips
'Gudoshnik', 'Ivory Florandale',
    'Oxford', and 'President Ken-
    nedy' Darwin hybrid tulips
'Bokara' Greigii tulip
'Queen of Sheba' lily-flowered
    tulip
'Aristocrat', 'Bond Street',
    'Flying Dutchman', 'Glacier',
    'Ivory Glory', and 'White
    Jewel' single-late tulips
'Black Parrot', 'Blue Parrot', and
    'Fantasy' parrot tulips

Rose Garden Summer Flowers

'Blue Bedder' mealycup
    sage
'Sincerity' and 'Snow Mass'
    geraniums
'Candidum' and 'Frieda Hemple'
    fancy-leaved caladiums
'Super Elfin White' impatiens
Lavender cotton
Catnip
Heliotrope
Dusty miller

Rose Garden Fall Flowers

'Late Giant' salvia
'Bronze Dot' tall button
    chrysanthemum
'Indian Summer' and
    'Pumpkin' giant harvest
    chrysanthemums
'Penguin' and 'Rollcall' cushion
    chrysanthemums

East Garden Spring Flowers

Garden thyme
Chives
Rosemary
Evergreen candytuft
Grape hyacinth
'Niphetos' single-late tulip
'Jewel of Spring' and
    'Sweet Harmony' Darwin
    hybrid tulips
'White Triumphator' lily-
    flowered tulip
'Faraday' parrot tulip
'Paydirt' pansy

East Garden Fall Flowers

'Victoria' mealycup sage
'Freedom' and 'White Patriot'
    cushion chrysanthemums
'Joanette' tubular petal
    chrysanthemum
'Starlet' spoon chrysanthemum

Garden Parties

Garden parties at the White House are always events with a magical sort of charm. Begun in the 1870s, they were held in May, usually once a week, and as a group of entertainments concluded the official social season in Washington, which began with the first state dinner at the White House in mid-December.

Victorian guests who had received engraved invitations entered through the North Portico and from the South Portico drank in a verdant scene. Blooming vines climbed the columns and the railings of the stairs that led down to the garden; tubs of spiky yucca, interplanted with geraniums and ferns, were set about. Men and women in crisp white and straw hats or parasols moved about over the carpet of rolled lawn to a receiving line, where the President's wife welcomed the guests one by one.

A canvas marquee, entwined with vines, was set up for punch, tea, and coffee. The leading pastry chef of

Easter egg rolling, originally held at the Capitol, was moved to the sloping South Lawn of the White House in the 1870s, when disgruntled members of Congress complained of little feet ruining the grass. This event, seen here about 1890 (right), contrasts with a serene garden party of 1884 (opposite), at which Chester A. Arthur greets his guests from the portico.

Washington, often the chocolatier Jules Demonet, had brought in a sumptuous spread of sweets, which he and the gardener arranged irresistibly with massed roses and orchids over white damask tablecloths. From one of the stairs of the South Portico the Marine Band serenaded, directed for much of the Victorian period by the march king John Philip Sousa.

The highlight of the occasion was the appearance of the President. This not being guaranteed, it remained something for the guests to hope for. He usually appeared on the portico and descended the stairs, from which he gave a little speech of greeting before mingling with the company.

The early garden parties were rather intimate, and young and old joined in relatively small numbers to enjoy the grounds and see who was to be seen. By 1900 invitations to a single party numbered as many as a thousand. Presidents had many people to recognize; by custom only a major personal disaster justified declining a White House invitation. The parties were streamlined: fewer sweets, a shorter concert, rarer visits from the President.

As regularly scheduled events they ended in the 1930s. Yet the tradition of the garden party never really died and prevails today. The President and First Lady are likely to invite 1,500 or 2,000 people to enjoy afternoon refreshments on the grounds in the spring, when the dogwood, redbud, and fruit trees are in bloom. ✌

GROVES

OF GREAT TREES

T he White House grounds are less a garden than a grove of great trees. "Trees tie it all down," says Irvin Williams, the grounds superinten- dent. All are cultivated to be nearly perfect specimens of their genus. Most were planted as young trees grown from seeds in the greenhouse or a propagating bed.

One of the largest trees ever planted at the White House was an eight-inch-diameter American elm installed by President Clinton in 1993 with the help of "Big John," a powerful, gaso- line-fueled tree spade. Like the Clinton elm, many of the White House trees were planted by the Presidents themselves to com- memorate their tenure or some historic event. Gerald Ford (1974–77), for example, planted an American elm beside the north driveway on the nation's 200th anniversary in 1976.

Tree planting was a concern, more than an interest, before the White House became the home of the President. Worried about the White House grounds, Secretary of the Navy Ben- jamin Stoddert wrote in 1800 from the capital in Philadelphia to William Thornton, a commissioner of the Federal city: "Trees should be planted at once, so as to make it an agreeable place to walk in." They were not to be until 1803, when Jeffer- son started his improvements; although he never completed this work, many seedlings were set out.

A watercolor painted in the 1820s suggests that Jefferson's plantings farthest to the east survived as an evergreen grove. The trees arranged in stiff, radial allées on the north, however, were gone by 1815, perhaps trampled in the War of 1812 by de- fending or invading soldiers or scorched in the terrible fire that consumed the house.

Following the reconstruction of the White House in 1818 during James Monroe's term, ambitious tree planting was car- ried out under a landscape plan by Charles Bulfinch, architect of the Capitol. Most of the documentation for this work is for areas outside the iron fence. Lafayette Park was planted in orchardlike rows with elm and cedar trees, in the hope that the cedars would grow up fast, giving an early show, and then could be cut when the slower-growing elms gained a presence.

John Quincy Adams's gardening tastes included trees. Hav- ing inspected forestry practices in Europe, he was one of the earliest proponents of forestry in the United States. Santa Rosa Forest, near Pensacola, Florida, was developed on his orders;

'An Agree- able Place to Walk In'

A handsome black gum tree (preceding pages), native to the area, dominates its corner of the southwest grounds; a silver atlas cedar lies beyond. Along the south driveway (opposite) a sugar maple shows its fall color, with 'Nellie Stevens' hollies nearby. The fountain is planted with canna lilies and scarlet salvia.

this plantation of more than 100,000 live oak trees was intended for the Navy's use in shipbuilding. With the oaks grown to giant scale and often bizarre form, it is a memorable sight today. An American elm attributed to Adams stood just southeast of the house until 1991, when, old and diseased, it had to be removed. White House gardeners, anticipating the end of the old elm, propagated a young tree from it, so a new Adams elm grows a few feet from the original planted by President Adams.

Tree planting at the White House resumed under Andrew Jackson in the 1830s and has never really stopped since then. The Irish-born James Maher, boisterous and convivial, was employed during Jackson's administration as public gardener for the city. His job was to beautify the public areas by grading the streets and public lands and by planting trees. Jefferson's poplars had grown old and brittle along the avenues; pedestrians complained of spiders and falling limbs. Many of the trees became victims of windstorms.

In 1831 Maher began replacing them with longer-lived oaks and sycamores along the southern perimeter of the President's Park. Maher maintained a private nursery across the river near Alexandria, which until 1846 was still a part of the District of Columbia. Here he cultivated numerous species of trees and sold them to the government, serving as both the seller and the buyer. Oaks, usually white oaks, were always first in favor. Oddly, he did not plant the American holly, which White House examples today show is acclimated splendidly to the region.

"Jemmy" Maher seems to have had no authority over the White House gardener, John Ousley, but they interacted frequently. Ousley, a quieter sort, stayed close to his White House work but made use of Maher's Alexandria nursery and was duly billed by Maher personally for plant material. Other plants came from some of the best nurseries in the United States, until 1850 still mostly on Long Island. Perhaps Ousley planted the *Magnolia grandiflora* known as the Andrew Jackson magnolia, which still grows on the south side of the White House.

In the early 1850s the celebrated landscape designer Andrew Jackson Downing was asked to improve the city's public lands. Had his plan been fully implemented, major tree planting and probably tree cutting would have occurred in the President's Park. Downing projected carefully defined groves of trees covering most of the White House grounds, with all plantings pulled away from the house. Under this plan, the house would have been viewed from Pennsylvania Avenue through trees—perhaps pruned upward to create a forestlike effect, with a cluster of trunks screening the mansion.

Early views trace the tree growth on the South Grounds, including the first known photograph (opposite top), taken in 1846, and one from seventy years later (opposite bottom) showing Woodrow Wilson's sheep. This horse chestnut (below) was pictured in a Dillon Marcus nursery catalogue about 1882, not long after Rutherford B. Hayes planted these trees in quantity at the White House.

It was a dramatic idea, but the groves were never planted. Not until twenty years later, when Ulysses Grant in 1871 ordered extensive improvements to the grounds, based more or less on Downing's designs, were the White House aspects of the plan undertaken. Even then, the concept was heavily edited. Some trees were planted, but hundreds more arrived in 1878 under the presidency of Rutherford B. Hayes. Based on early photographs, they were sizable specimens eight to ten feet tall, sometimes larger. In addition to the usual oaks, Hayes planted spruces and firs, the bluish, dense trees that recall mountainous country and do well in Washington's climate.

Hayes, who loved commemorations of all kinds, introduced the commemorative tree, an idea that was to come into its own in the next century. He wanted a tree to represent each President and his state, as well as each state in the Union. The grounds were given a plentiful supply of Ohio buckeyes (horse chestnuts) to honor Hayes's native state. In the quantity he selected he was prophetic: Hayes was the third of the Ohio Presidents, and four more were yet to come. On the North Grounds, the buckeyes lining the driveway lived to a brittle old age, the last blowing over in a storm during World War II.

For fifty years after Hayes few important changes took place. Evergreen shrubbery was continually planted to set off the whiteness of the house and to give structure to the landscape. In Lafayette Park, Bulfinch's elm trees began to die after forty

Magnolias through time:
The Jackson magnolia's ancient
limbs frame the windows of
the Blue Room (opposite).
Workers pause for a chat on
the south driveway about
1875, with the Jackson
magnolia in the distance
(above left). A magnolia from
the Wilson Administration
was saved by Harry Truman
and moved to a new location
in 1952 (above right).

years, and the square became an open place with grass and shrubbery, not the groves of trees with bisecting walks originally projected.

Photographs taken in the 1880s and 1890s show the White House enveloped in shade. Trees planted in the times of both Grant and Hayes covered the South Grounds. They do not appear to have been trimmed much but were allowed to take their natural shapes. Their random locations gave an old-fashioned, rather pastoral appearance to the grounds on the south, whereas on the north the trees were planted in lines to some extent, evidence of which survives today.

The next serious alteration of the grounds after Hayes came more than a half century later, with a plan in the 1930s by Frederick Law Olmsted Jr. featuring trees. When the plan was rejuvenated in the early 1960s, the contemporary taste for mass planting was avoided in favor of a natural and woods-like use of trees, seen in the White House grounds today.

Some eighteen acres are contained within the iron fence. More than five hundred trees, all splendid specimens, thrive here. Forty-one are commemoratives, including the famous magnolia planted by Andrew Jackson probably in the 1830s.

Today's green apples (above) do not rival those of the old tree (right), possibly a gift of Andrew Jackson Downing: it produced three varieties annually for eighty years. Elsewhere on the South Grounds (opposite), an American cork tree shares the lawn with an old Japanese tree lilac planted before 1900.

This venerable tree, which in June is laden with cream-colored blossoms, was given special protection from construction and falling debris during the White House renovations of 1948–52; it was frozen while in its winter dormancy, extracted from the ground, and temporarily planted in a safe place. Afterward, it was returned to its approximate historic site, where it survives today in a cat's cradle of supporting cables.

This *Magnolia grandiflora* variety is especially popular in Washington, although it can have a hard time this far north unless it has access to sun on winter days. Prolonged freezes and strong, cold winds will kill it back to its trunk or to the ground. Other magnolias, such as the *soulangiana* and the *soulangiana* 'Alba', have been popular White House commemoratives, but these saucer magnolias are likely to be nipped in their first bloom in late March or early April. Oaks also rank high as commemoratives, including the pin oak, northern red oak, white oak, willow oak, and scarlet oak. Dogwood, linden, pine, beech, elm, and Japanese maples are other favorites. To this relatively small number, add the rest of the five hundred trees and the White House grounds are an arboretum of extraordinary extent.

Southeast of the house stands one bur oak of unknown origin, but it is very large and thus probably very old. This may be the finest specimen anywhere of one of the noblest species of oak. Old paulownia trees, treasured in Asia for their wood,

In the fall an American elm at the Southeast Gate sheds its leaves (opposite). A magnificent Japanese threadleaf maple (below left), planted in 1893 by Frances Cleveland, graces the south fountain area. Roots from a large sycamore tree were spared and carefully wrapped when a utility ditch was dug in 1950 (below right).

show lavender blossoms in the spring; with their twisted trunks and fingerlike leaves, they and the atlas cedars seem to be exotic visitors among the native American trees. Elms on the North Lawn have grown to enormous size and, like umbrellas, shade a level lawn and a fountain.

The trees "require very high maintenance," observes Irvin Williams. Their survival is well assured in the White House landscaping program. They are fed every three years with a staggering variety of nutrients. Most have copper cabling to lightning rods in their upper limbs. Seeds, cuttings, or grafts start new plantings that will one day—far ahead in many cases—replace the old. "Propagation is a major part of our philosophy," Williams says. "We have good, strong plants and develop good strong plants from them."

The trees are an unsung glory, giving the White House landscape its structure. Living things that they are, they express on yet another level the continuity of this place through time. Generations of trees have been planted, grown, and died. New generations always replace them. One moonlit evening during the Civil War Walt Whitman strolled by the White House and was moved to write a poem about the "soft transparent, hazy, thin, blue moon-lace" leaf shadows made on the "tall round columns, spotless as snow." The effect can still be seen on luminous Washington nights.

Panoramic views of the North Lawn during Franklin D. Roosevelt's administration (above and below) show both horse chestnut and elm trees, many of which have since died. In winter, the limbs of the elms near the North Portico become merely black outlines against the white snow (opposite).

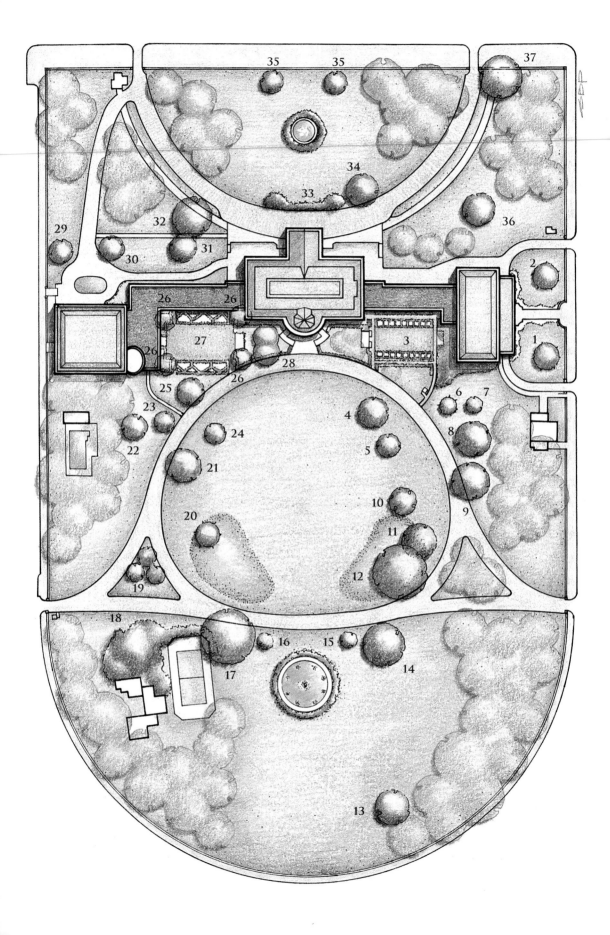

Although earlier Presidents planted trees, the custom of commemorative trees on the White House grounds probably began with President Hayes in the late 1870s, inspired by the nation's centennial, and was enthusiastically followed in the twentieth century. There are now forty-one commemoratives:

1. SOUTHERN MAGNOLIA
   Franklin D. Roosevelt (1942)
2. SOUTHERN MAGNOLIA
   Warren G. Harding (1922, replaced 1947)
3. EAST GARDEN (1965)
4. WILLOW OAK
   Ronald Reagan (1988)
5. LITTLELEAF LINDEN
   George Bush and Elizabeth II (1991)
6. WHITE PINE
   Gerald R. Ford (1977)
7. EASTERN REDBUD
   George Bush (1990)
8. NORTHERN RED OAK
   Dwight D. Eisenhower (1959)
9. PATMORE ASH
   George Bush (1989)
10. WHITE DOGWOOD
    Bill and Hillary Clinton (1995)
11. PURPLE BEECH
    George Bush (1991)
12. AMERICAN ELM
    John Q. Adams (original 1826), Barbara Bush (1991)
13. WHITE OAK
    Herbert Hoover (1935)
14. WILLOW OAK
    Bill and Hillary Clinton (1993)
15. JAPANESE MAPLE
    Rosalynn Carter (1978)
16. JAPANESE THREADLEAF MAPLE
    Frances Folsom Cleveland (1893)
17. AMERICAN ELM
    Bill and Hillary Clinton (1993)
18. CHILDREN'S GARDEN (1969)
19. WHITE DOGWOODS (3)
    Hillary Rodham Clinton (1994)
20. CEDAR-OF-LEBANON
    Jimmy Carter (1978)
21. WHITE OAK
    Herbert Hoover (1931)
22. PIN OAK
    Dwight D. Eisenhower (1958)
23. LITTLELEAF LINDEN
    Bill Clinton (1993)
24. LITTLELEAF LINDEN
    Franklin D. Roosevelt (1937)
25. WILLOW OAK
    Lyndon B. Johnson (1964)
26. SAUCER MAGNOLIAS (4)
    John F. Kennedy (1962)
27. ROSE GARDEN (1913)
28. SOUTHERN MAGNOLIAS (2)
    Andrew Jackson (1830)
29. SUGAR MAPLE
    Ronald Reagan (1984)
30. FERNLEAF BEECH
    Patricia Nixon (1972)
31. FERNLEAF BEECH
    Lady Bird Johnson (1968)
32. AMERICAN ELM
    Betty Ford (1975)
33. AMERICAN AND ENGLISH BOXWOOD
    Harry S. Truman (1952)
34. RED MAPLE
    Jimmy Carter (1977)
35. WHITE SAUCER MAGNOLIAS (2)
    Nancy Reagan (1982)
36. WHITE OAK
    Franklin D. Roosevelt (1935)
37. SCARLET OAK
    Benjamin Harrison (1889)

Commemorative Trees

The more than three dozen commemoratives are only a small portion of the White House trees, but they are among the most venerable. The drawing opposite locates all the trees planted by the Presidents and First Ladies on the North and South Grounds.

Christmas Trees and Holiday Decorations

At Christmas the White House dresses up. An eighteen-foot tree in the Blue Room (right) is only the beginning. The entire house is festive with seasonal decorations, such as a cranberry cone set on conifer branches on a Red Room table (opposite).

However they use flowers, no President in the last thirty years has settled for less than splendid decorations at Christmas. The season at the White House is introduced by the forty-two-foot National Christmas Tree on the Ellipse, a living tree that was transported from Pennsylvania and planted full grown. One gardener commented at the time that its ball of dirt was so large "the tree never knew it left home."

The first National Christmas Tree was put up by Calvin Coolidge in 1923. For Christmas 1941 security considerations in the wake of Pearl Harbor caused the tree to be moved into the confines of the South Lawn, where the President, by tradition, pushed the button to light it. That Christmas, when FDR lighted the tree from the South Portico, British Prime Minister Winston Churchill's was among the faces on which its glare shone. He had arrived secretly to meet with the President about the war just declared.

From then on the National Christmas Tree was cut in November in one of the states and brought to Washington. In 1954 President Dwight D. Eisenhower requested a permanent tree for the north end of the Ellipse. The first did not live long, and those that followed have not thrived either, given their large size. The most recent tree, however, planted in 1978, has with help prospered.

Interior trees probably began with Benjamin Harrison (1889–93), who set up one for his grandchildren during their first Christmas at the White House. None is known to have been decorated after that until Theodore Roosevelt's time, when his children put up a tree and he used Christmas-tree centerpieces on tables at a dance in 1908. The Tafts decorated a tree in the Blue Room in 1910. Calvin Coolidge's outdoor tree was continued by Herbert Hoover (1929–33), but Lou Henry Hoover also placed a Christmas tree in the south end of the State Dining Room— apparently launching the unbroken tradition of a tree inside the White House.

Each year a Christmas tree is placed in the Blue Room. Workers remove the chandelier, and the eighteen-foot tree takes its place in the center of the oval space. Hundreds of ornaments mingle with a thousand lights. In 1995 architects and architecture students contributed 608 miniature structures to depict the theme "'Twas the Night Before Christmas."

Elsewhere the White House is decorated for Christmas according to the First Lady's wishes. Whatever special decorations are devised for any given year, there are often potted poinsettias, brought from the greenhouse and arranged on hearths and placed on pyramids in the hall. ❧

SHAPING

THE GROUNDS

Managing
the Garden

Those who live and work at the White House have a personal relationship with the garden. A chef gathers ingredients from the Herb Garden for a state dinner (above right). Presidents' grandchildren have impressed their hands and feet in the paths of the Children's Garden (below right). Comfortable patio furniture is arranged outside the Oval Office, overlooking the Rose Garden (opposite).

98

Managing the White House grounds is a complicated, highly organized business. Yet in a sense it is as personal as cultivating one's own yard. The territory here may be larger, but each part is managed somewhat unto itself. Early in his term, in 1961, John F. Kennedy declined to designate the White House a National Historic Landmark, but he did define the President's Park as Reservation One of the National Park Service and charged the Park Service with its maintenance.

The various gardens—the East Garden, the West or Rose Garden, the Children's Garden—have their particular needs for pruning, mulching, and replanting. The first two are nearly a century old and, although redesigned several times, retain the flavor of early American gardens. The Children's Garden, added by Lady Bird Johnson in 1969, is a secluded playground retreat for White House youngsters, situated on the lower part of the South Lawn. Jimmy Carter (1977–81) encouraged the Herb Garden, of which the White House chef makes frequent use.

The White House garden command center is a small office beneath the green turf of the North Lawn. On its cinder-block walls are maps of the grounds, schedules, and remedies. Head gardeners have been surprisingly few over the years. They usually have long careers in the job, becoming devoted to the challenging care of a garden that must always be perfect.

The present head gardener, Irvin Williams, joined the White House in 1961. His tenure has been one of the longest. Predecessors include Robert Redmond, who came in 1923 and stayed forty years. John Ousley held the title from John Quincy Adams's administration to Franklin Pierce's, and Henry Pfister served the presidencies of Rutherford Hayes to Theodore Roosevelt.

I t is unlikely that a single square inch of the White House acreage remains as it was when the house was constructed. The grounds have been built up for nearly two centuries to fill swamps and keep the ground rich. Through the first half of the nineteenth century, filling and grading outside the iron fence of the White House created a nearly continuous rhythm of change in the President's Park.

L'Enfant's plan of 1792, kept tacked up on the office wall of the commissioner of public buildings, was generally the guide for what to do. Where vagaries intervened, appropriate alternatives were agreed on with a nod or handshake. But by the time Washington had been occupied for half a century, the plan seemed impossible to complete.

The capital had not become the metropolis of the first President's dream. Town life was densely clustered in some places and dispersed in others, with hundreds of vacant lots. Dirt streets met paved streets. Dingy alleys served as close-in residential neighborhoods for the poor.

New direction came along in 1850. On the death of Zachary Taylor that July, Vice President Millard Fillmore took office to find the Army Corps of Engineers about to embark on major improvements in the city. A surveyor in his youth, Fillmore (1850–53) took an interest in land and planning and was in step with modern landscape gardening ideas. Encouraged by local citizens, the President made public works a high priority. First, he invited America's leading architect, Thomas U. Walter of Philadelphia, to take over the expansion of the Capitol. Second, he engaged the famous landscape gardener and author Andrew Jackson Downing to make a landscape plan for the President's Park and the Mall.

For Downing the commission was an opportunity. Demanding the title "rural architect," he took on the project with zeal, eager to make Washington a showcase for the ideas he espoused in his popular books, notably *A Treatise on the Theory and Practice of Landscape Gardening* (1841). He recommended an almost complete departure from L'Enfant's plan. Within the classical outlines already built, he redesigned open public areas as deep, picturesque woodlands threaded by winding walks and driveways that offered endless numbers of beautiful landscape scenes.

The Plan Takes Root

The south fountain (pages 96–97) was built in 1871 on orders from President Grant, its water spray powered by steam. To its right is one of the most memorable sights in the garden, the Japanese threadleaf maple added in 1893. From the south the White House (opposite), built of dressed stone and surrounded by greenery, resembles a sculpture in its own garden.

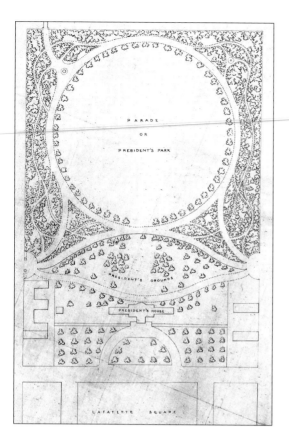

Downing scorned the obsolescence and foreignness of the L'Enfant plan, although his own concept reflected some of the same precepts. He borrowed freely from the English picturesque landscape movement that had provided models for Washington and Jefferson. Even though Downing's death in an 1852 steamboat explosion generally devastated the new plan, aspects of his landscape philosophy lived on in Washington. "My object," he wrote, "is to form a collection of all the trees that will grow in the climate of Washington . . . to form a public museum of living trees and shrubs. . . ." The city's devotion today to specimen trees can be attributed to Downing.

Returned to the engineers, the plan was undertaken piecemeal. For the President's Park, the main changes came in the introduction of thick groves of trees and the design for a circular parade ground where the now-filled marshes along Tiber Creek had been and where the Ellipse would be built twenty years later. Trees were planted with security in mind, to frame views of the house but leave space all around it that could be patrolled on foot or guarded from the windows and roof. A screen of trees was planned for the north side, by the portico, but it resulted only in an ineffectual, snaggled barrier of crooked pines. Little of the plan was accomplished, because political storms and ultimately the Civil War overshadowed it. Fillmore, the patron, left office in 1853.

The house that greeted Abraham Lincoln in 1861 looked about as it had for a decade. On the north, between the two arms of the driveway, Lincoln saw an iron-fenced garden planted with a few roses alongside a gravel path. In the center stood the full-length bronze figure of Thomas Jefferson by David d'Angenou that James K. Polk had placed there in 1848.

Lincoln's numerous callers were unable to venture from the driveway or beyond the iron railings, and they had no means of entry from the south. The gates at the street were locked at sundown. New gates had been built on the sides and were also kept locked, although Cabinet members had keys. Near the close of Lincoln's administration, Maj. B. B. French, the public buildings commissioner, built a fountain on the South Lawn, a fanciful arrangement of terra-cotta bowls held up by dolphins, but the major was never able to make the jet spray properly.

Andrew Jackson Downing, a giant in the history of American landscape design, provided a plan for the White House that featured a formal parade to the south. Modified in later years, his idea became the Ellipse.

After the Civil War, in the period known as the Gilded Age, petunias and ferns brimmed in the window boxes and cast-iron urns of row houses facing Lafayette Park. Ulysses Grant in the 1870s banished all plans to relocate the White House and within a few years was calling for improvements. Most were in the interest of privacy and included building carriage driveways in an area that could be enclosed beyond the iron fence south of the White House. Gen. Orville E. Babcock, a close friend and private secretary for the first two years of the administration, became Grant's public buildings commissioner and took on the project with zeal. An army engineer, Babcock had been with General Grant at Appomattox.

One of his first jobs at the White House was to direct the restoration of the flower garden on each side of the South Portico. Exactly when this garden of meandering paths was established is not known. A fence divided it from the driveway. Perhaps the parterre was created to receive some of the plant material when the old garden was demolished in 1857. An official wrote of the garden in July 1860, "No one enters the parterres except members of the family and I presume they but seldom, as I have never seen anyone in them." Grant and his immediate successor, Rutherford B. Hayes (1877–81), especially enjoyed this garden and made it a feature of lawn parties.

East and West Executive Avenues were built to the sides of the White House in 1866 and 1871, separating the residence from the expanded Treasury Building on the east and the new State, War and Navy Building under construction on the west. Jefferson's East Wing, demolished by Andrew Johnson, was replaced by a low, columned porch that had no public function—it opened only into the service basement—but was an architectural feature for that end of the house, to be viewed over a large round pool.

General Babcock moved the iron fence a few hundred yards to the south, to approximately its present location, and built the first circular pool there. Seventy-five feet in diameter, it featured a "French gurg," a steam pump that spewed water from a ball of short, reedlike fountain heads, making a heavy spray and mist. For the area south of the fence, where the Civil War stockyards had been, he took Downing's scheme and in conference with Grant decided on a guitar-shaped driveway or promenade on the new ground,

The first White House fountain (below), installed on the South Lawn in 1865, is shown in this photograph from about 1866. The Andrew Jackson magnolia, just left of the portico, is in its formative years. Before the North Portico was built (following pages), the North Grounds had various configurations: the area in Abraham Lincoln's time (page 104, top), as Ulysses S. Grant knew it (center), and in William McKinley's time (bottom). Today the fountain boasts changing settings to take full advantage of each season's bounty (page 105).

In 1868 Andrew Johnson demolished Thomas Jefferson's East Colonnade and created this side entrance to the South Grounds, designed by Alfred B. Mullett, architect of the Treasury. The original colonnade was reconstructed in 1902.

instead of the circle suggested by Downing. Some grading was accomplished but stopped abruptly when Babcock was implicated in the Whiskey Ring scandal of 1872. Without Babcock, the gardening projects slowly fizzled out.

In the nineteenth century the grounds of the White House were kept faithfully but not always creatively, unless the President himself was interested. Old photographs and documents tell of the regular gardening routine established by Babcock in Grant's time. A mule-drawn mower cut the high grass shaggy as farmers do with hay. Laborers followed the mower, flattening the stubble with a lawn roller. Spray from the garden watering machine, which resembled a small fire engine with a manual pump, provided a general greening.

When he came to office after Grant in 1877, President Hayes

found many projects half done. He set the engineers to work again on the land south of the fence. With his personal encouragement—and some of his own money—the landscape was brought to completion between July 1879 and September 1880. Hundreds of wagonloads of dirt were carried in to raise the ground level. The guitar-shaped driveway became a long graveled oval, known ultimately as the Ellipse, and the seventeen-acre park was raised probably seven feet above what it had been in Washington's day and planted heavily with elm trees. The Ellipse was virtually taken over by Washingtonians as a promenade and carriage drive. By providing such a fine public area, a security-conscious President was able to further limit public access within the iron fence without appearing inhospitable.

Little was done to change the grounds following Hayes's departure. Plan after plan was rejected over the years for lack of funding. Two and three decades into the twentieth century, benign neglect had resulted in shrubbery too big, trees out of shape, and hedges indulged to bulbousness. The problem lay not in an abuse of nature but in its too generous accommodation. Eleanor Roosevelt asked in 1933 that her grandchildren's swing be mounted to a tree limb. When her request was denied as being bad for the tree, it became clear that change was on the way.

Franklin Delano Roosevelt (1933–45) liked to make plans for houses. Better known for inventing new rooms, such as the White House library, and for expanding the West Wing in 1934 and the East Wing in 1942, he was interested in doing what was right for the grounds. His severe allergies perhaps denied him a lifetime dedication to gardening, but while he was President he was dubiously honored when a willowlike member of the sunflower family *(Baccharis neglecta)* became known as the New Deal or Roosevelt weed.

The President invited Frederick Law Olmsted Jr. to solve the problem of the White House grounds, aware that his expert was the premier designer of public spaces in the country. Son of the famous planner of New York's Central Park, Olmsted had continued Olmsted Brothers in Brookline, Massachusetts, after the death of his father, increasing its renown as a leading landscape architecture firm. The company's 1902 garden plan, made for Theodore Roosevelt at the instigation of the architect Charles McKim, had been tabled for lack of both interest and funding. Knowing the second Roosevelt's liking for history and eager to do the job, Olmsted engaged the services of Morley Jeffers Williams, a professor in the School of Landscape Architecture at Harvard University, to research the subject and assist with his recommendations to the White House. Williams

An early project of about 1878 for the Ellipse, during the administration of Rutherford B. Hayes, organized the unhealthy swamp into a park with tree-lined drives. The plan was generally realized by 1880.

was then in the process of restoring George Washington's garden at Mount Vernon.

Olmsted toured the grounds in 1935, making notes. The 1850s parterres against the south of the house were still in place, complete to their iron fence, albeit buried in honeysuckle, clematis, and tangled roses. He marveled at the giant trees and puzzled over the odd mixture of elements from various periods. The President wanted the landscape put under some overall concept. Olmsted's solution for the White House began as a report. Later the firm made actual plans, which were followed bit by bit over the next half century, but the concept made the difference. It is the key to the design of the grounds today.

First Olmsted envisioned the South Grounds as a parklike setting. All flower beds, little gardens and plantings, and other interruptions to this idea were to be omitted. The grounds in general were to present a planted and carefully maintained grove of trees, cut through by a broad, open southward vista. Thickened groves along the sides would screen the view from nearby streets, and from the end one could see the White House at the top of the sloping lawn. Driveways that crossed this lawn were to be sunken to avoid visually interrupting the sweep of green grass. The north side would retain its elms and oaks and remain a shady lawn, seen from a closer proximity than the south. Parking was to be taken off all driveways. An added feature was the plan's reverse view, from the White House out. The tranquil Jefferson Memorial eventually climaxed the mighty vista in 1943.

Formal gardens under Olmsted's plan were to be confined to those areas beside the wings where they already existed. Olmsted recommended that both the East and West Gardens be carefully thought out and redesigned in a formal, almost austere manner. Although there were more details to his recommendations, these were the essentials. Over time the scheme has been developed carefully. The groves that flank the South Lawn are mature today and screen the lawn from the street.

The Presidents since Franklin Roosevelt have all given their support to the ideas expressed in the Olmsted plan. It is flexible. Change usually fits somehow. The care and maintenance of existing plant material extend to an active propagation program, including the gathering of seeds, grafting, and rooting. Over the past thirty years, for the first time in their history, the White House grounds have achieved a venerable, even mellow quality that characterizes old gardens and that new gardens never have. The genius of this is Olmsted's plan, developed six decades ago.

The fountain on the south (below) stands in the sloping and gardenesque vista that stretches from the White House to the Jefferson Memorial (opposite). Pierre Charles L'Enfant had anticipated this effect, although envisioning a greater distance and a pyramid as the focal point.

The Swamp to the South

English engravers in the 1830s produced this romanticized view of the White House from the south. In fact the placid river in the foreground was the angry Tiber Creek, and a swamp separated it from the high ground on which the White House stood.

Before the President's Park south of the White House was filled in, it exuded a swampy smell and a pale fog rose from it on fall and late winter mornings. Thomas Jefferson stood at his office windows and watched the fog crawling toward the White House, convinced that it brought death. He wrote to his daughter on April 25, 1803: "I wish you to come as early as possible; because, though the members of the Government remain here to the last week in July, yet the sickly season commences, in fact, by the middle of that month, and it would not be safe for you to keep the children here."

James Madison was the first to remain at the White House in the summer. That was in 1814, and he fled ahead of the invading British, who

burned the White House. The vapors do not seem to have done the frail Madison any harm. William Henry Harrison's death in 1841 was blamed on the foul air from the marsh even though he was physically fit and died in early spring. When ex-President James K. Polk died suddenly in Nashville in 1849, three months after he moved home, he was believed a certain victim of the poison because he had remained at the White House every summer of his administration.

To escape the marsh and the almost unbearable heat of July and August, early Presidents usually left Washington for the summer. When the press of business eventually made long absences impossible, alternatives to staying in the White House were found. In the late 1830s Martin Van Buren rented a house in the suburbs, several miles from the White House. For the official summer residence, a sickly James Buchanan in 1857 enlisted the Soldier's Home, just outside town. The rambling, vine-hung cottage served Lincoln and was used in summers until 1881, when improved railroads shortened the distance to the healthy salt air of the Jersey shore. ✸

RESIDENT'S PARK

Most gardening activity at the White House is not seen by the public or anyone but the gardening staff. Every effort is made to ensure that work inside the iron fence passes unseen. Walking along the fence, one can sometimes catch a glimpse of a flower bed being prepared, a tree being pruned, or grass being mowed.

In the rest of the President's Park, however, the public can move about at will, so gardening is conducted in full view. It is natural that visitors have an avid curiosity about what goes on inside the fence. Yet the delights of the public areas beyond the fence are many.

The White House garden extended—the President's Park—includes the entire original grounds of the President's House, as designed by L'Enfant. Some other parts, previously taken away, have come again into the President's complex. A brief tour of this territory follows.

East and West. Of the four Federal departments that have occupied the President's Park since 1800, only the Treasury, east of the White House, remains. On the west, the departments of State, War, and Navy moved elsewhere early in the twentieth century, freeing the mighty Second Empire–style building of the 1870s, which had housed all three, as offices for the Executive Branch of the government. The property west of the White House thus has been returned to the fold.

North. Pennsylvania Avenue first crossed the President's Park in 1822 and was closed to vehicular traffic in 1995. Across the avenue, to the north, is Lafayette Park, planned in 1821 by the architect Charles Bulfinch and several years later, on completion, named for the first foreign guest of state to stay in the White House, General Lafayette. Before that, the area had been called the common, reserved for market fairs and similar events, but it was part of the White House grounds.

Of special interest on the north side of the White House is the iron fence itself. Designed and built in 1818, it has remained much the same since, except that in 1831 Andrew Jackson ordered the great stone piers rolled on logs farther apart and the curve of the horseshoe-shaped drive widened to better accommodate carriages. Nearly all parts of the fence have been

Outside the Iron Fence

Thomas Eakins's painting of the view from the Hayes family quarters (preceding pages), from about 1880, shows the Victorian affection for forestlike settings of trees, a taste that lives on at the White House. From the second-story window where Abraham Lincoln used to give his speeches (opposite), one looks north to Lafayette Park and on up Sixteenth Street, a surviving element of L'Enfant's grand vision.

replaced with copies of the original, some in steel, but original gates were in place on the northwest as late as 1976. Originals of the lanterns on the gateposts were put up in 1858, provided by Cornelius and Baker of Philadelphia, and burned gas.

Lafayette Park has been crowned since 1853 by Clark Mills's equestrian statue in bronze of Gen. Andrew Jackson, hero of the 1815 Battle of New Orleans and later President. The first equestrian statue cast in the United States, it was created at Mills's temporary studio and furnace only a block away. Around the statue's base are four eighteenth-century Spanish cannon captured by Jackson in the Florida campaign of 1819. On the granite base of the statue is Jackson's famous toast, challenging nullifiers, "Our Federal Union. It must be preserved!" This was omitted when the statue was dedicated in 1853, to satisfy the building committee chairman, Sen. Jefferson Davis.

Other statuary around Lafayette Park includes, at the four corners, bronze groups honoring foreign heroes of the American Revolution. On the southeast corner is General Lafayette (1891), by Jean Alexandre Joseph Falquière and Marius Jean Antonin Mercié; on the southwest is Maj. Gen. Comte Jean de Rochambeau (1902), by J. J. Fernand Hamar; on the northeast is Brig. Gen. Thaddeus Kosciuszko (1910), by Antoni Popiel; and on the northwest is Maj. Gen. Friedrich Wilhelm von Steuben (1910), by Albert Jaegers.

Two large vases to the south may have been designed by Andrew Jackson Downing or his partner, Calvert Vaux. They were cast at the Navy Yard in 1872 by Navy employees, using melted cannon from the Civil War. They appear in Downing's plan, flanking the Jackson statue, but were moved to their present locations in 1936. Since the late 1870s, during President Hayes's time, they have been planted in vines and flowers.

Lafayette Park was once a prime residential address. In 1845 an act of Congress paved the way to build official residences for the Cabinet along its facing side streets, Jackson Place and Madison Place. Legislation eighty years later cleared the way for replacement of the old houses with Federal high-rise office buildings. Franklin Roosevelt's rescue of Blair House (1824) on Pennsylvania Avenue as a guest residence during World War II did not entirely halt the demolition plans.

Only in 1962, in part through the intervention of Jacqueline Kennedy, was the office-block movement halted and the nineteenth-century domestic character of the buildings preserved. Rowhouse facades—some old, some new—now screen the modern office buildings behind, bringing back the square's domestic character. Still lining Lafayette Park are Commodore

Sculpture in the President's Park includes Clark Mills's Andrew Jackson (1853) (above); Daniel Chester French's First Division Monument (1924) (opposite top); the Sherman Monument (1903), by Carl Rohl-Smith et al. (center); and the granite fountain (1913) dedicated to Francis Davis Millet and Archibald Butt (bottom), also by Daniel Chester French.

Stephen Decatur's mansion and Dolley Madison's house, but regal residences by architects such as H. H. Richardson and James Renwick have been destroyed over the years.

South. The southern part of the President's Park is the Ellipse, a large open area surrounded by oval drives. Its development began in the 1850s but was cut short first by a lack of funds and then by the Civil War, when it had horse pens and a slaughter house. In 1871, in President Grant's era, the White House grounds were extended beyond Jefferson's stone wall and an iron fence defined the circular southern extreme. E Street was built between the fence and the Ellipse, which was under improvement for the next twenty years as it was filled, graded, and planted with hundreds of trees.

Just south of the Old Executive Office Building is the gold-plated bronze First Division Monument of World War I (1924), by Daniel Chester French, its base column by Cass Gilbert and his son, the architect Cass Gilbert Jr. Opposite this on the east, across the President's Park near Fifteenth Street, is the William Tecumseh Sherman Monument (1903), by Carl Rohl-Smith and others. Within view, on the south front of the Treasury, is James Earle Fraser's full-length statue of Alexander Hamilton (1923) on a base designed by Henry Bacon, architect of the Lincoln Memorial.

The Ellipse also features the Boy Scout Memorial (1964), a sculpture group in bronze by Donald DeLue. Here also is the zero milestone, from which all distance from the city is measured. Near Constitution Avenue is the Second Division Memorial (1936), by James Earle Fraser, with its golden flaming sword and a base by John Russell Pope, architect of the Jefferson Memorial. A small marble cenotaph (1936) by Carl Mose is dedicated to the planters of this area who sold their land to the government to create the District of Columbia.

The two sandstone buildings of neoclassical design at the south end of the park at Fifteenth and Seventeenth Streets are gate lodges from the Capitol, built about 1828 by Charles Bulfinch and moved here in 1880 when the elder Frederick Law Olmsted landscaped the Capitol.

All of this is part of the President's Park, to which the White House and its iron-fenced grounds are central. Outside the fence, the amount of land once again under White House jurisdiction and use is surprisingly large, including the Old Executive Office Building, East and West Executive Avenues, Pennsylvania Avenue, Lafayette Park, and Jackson Place. All today are more part of the White House than of the city.

T*he earliest Presidents shared the taste of the late eighteenth and nineteenth centuries for picturesque landscapes. In their letters Jefferson and Washington called this "English gardening." But while the groves of the White House garden are picturesque and forestlike, the grounds are not like a traditional English garden. The best description is not a label: the grounds are unique to the White House and have become over time what they are, the ideas of many people.*

The first President's ambitions for the house and its park were higher than even he believed might be realized. But visions too broad never troubled him. George Washington's park was to be a place to use, with cool groves and stretches of high wavy grass; paths for long walks and horseback rides; creek banks for contemplation, picnicking, and fly fishing. Part might have been formally landscaped, leaving the rest a "wilderness." Washington approved L'Enfant's plan for grand terraces and pools.

It is not difficult to paint a picture of what an eighteenth-century country man like Washington might have wanted in such a sprawling park surrounding his house. Imagine in the eighty-two acres a park where wild deer roam, protected for beauty and a ready supply of presidential venison. Much of the land is devoted to woods managed for firewood. Nearer the house, parterres of vegetables and flowers fill out the picture. There are orchards abounding in fruits; yellow stacks of hay in summer and autumn meadows; and a botanical garden, so that the President can enjoy specimen plants and trees.

Instead of this picturesque park, the grounds developed less stringently fixed on a single concept than as front and back yards for the Presidents. Everyone who has cared to do so—Presidents and First Ladies—has left a mark. John Quincy Adams created a "gardener's garden," Grant parterres, and Hayes the Ellipse. Edith Roosevelt contributed a colonial garden and Ellen Wilson a rose garden. Franklin Roosevelt opened up a vista to the new Jefferson Memorial; Lady Bird Johnson established the Children's Garden. There are numerous trees by which to remember people and events. All of these are alterations, some significant, others barely noticed.

Change is inevitable in landscapes. Trees die; freezes cut plants to the ground. Innovation enters. Americans thrive on

A Hardy Survivor

Moon Ring 3, *a sculpture in Texas granite by Jesus Bautista Moroles, on loan from the Old Jail Art Center, Albany, Texas, has been part of the East Garden sculpture exhibitions during the Clinton Administration.*

The 'Alexandrina' saucer magnolia in front of the West Wing is one of four that form the corners of the Rose Garden (above). A scarlet oak, to the left, and a horse chestnut stand shoulder to shoulder in the snow (opposite).

new things. For all its transformations, however, no American landscape has been kept for so long in such a high state of maintenance as the White House grounds. When the capital was young, the White House loomed over its park and could be seen for several miles away, from across the river or the rooftops of the nascent cityscape. Most of the acreage of the President's Park was surrendered to other purposes, a process that started early. Time has seen the modern city swarm around the White House and transform its quiet neighborhood into a commercial downtown. The massiveness of the house shrinks before high-rises.

Franklin Roosevelt closed West Executive Avenue in 1941 for wartime security. East Executive Avenue was made into a pedestrian way in 1987. President Clinton barred vehicular traffic from Pennsylvania Avenue in 1995—the most radical of all the security closings because the avenue in these blocks was a principal transportation artery in the city. North and south, H and E Streets remain open to traffic. Across Lafayette Park, the view of the White House from H Street is fleeting but always charming at night and more so in rain or snow. On E Street one can only drive by in a car, slow briefly, and look up the green vista to the back side of the house before being urged to resume rolling.

If something has been lost with the closed streets, unquestionably more has been gained. The White House now functions more effectively in accommodating its varied activities. Security is tighter, but visitors are able to enjoy at least some of the White House and its grounds any time of the day on foot or seated on benches. The space is vast, shady with trees, and welcoming in a way it was not when cars and trucks poured through it in a never-ending flow.

Lafayette Park always attracts people. At times it is a political hotplate. Even on ordinary days it is odd to see. In the midst of fountains, bronze statuary, and elm trees, noisy protesters wield painted signs and bullhorns and sometimes pause to play chess at lunchtime with brown-bagging Federal office workers or the homeless, before resuming their labors, protected by the First Amendment.

Over the past half century the White House has had to reclaim some of the lost parts of the President's Park. Some day it may in one way or another take the rest. The President's Park, like the White House itself, is an amazing survivor in a culture so enamored of rebuilding that it sometimes lacks the wisdom to preserve. The White House and its landscape have prevailed together, surviving in their different ways—both symbols of state and timeless reminders of the nation's long duration.

Chronology

1790 A site for the new national capital is selected along the Potomac River

1791 Working with George Washington, Pierre Charles L'Enfant prepares a city plan for Washington, D.C., reserving eighty-two acres for a "President's park"

1792 The "President's palace" is sited; L'Enfant's grand scheme is replaced by James Hoban's plan for the present White House; construction of the house begins

1797 Plans for Federal office buildings to be built on each side of the White House mark the first intrusions into the President's Park

1800 John Adams is the first President to occupy the White House and orders a garden

1801 Thomas Jefferson undertakes new plans for the garden, including a stone wall around the house; he plants numerous trees about 1802–6

1814 The British burn the White House in the War of 1812

1818 As the White House is rebuilt, James Monroe increases tree planting based on plans by Charles Bulfinch

1818 Iron gates are installed on the north driveway

1822 Pennsylvania Avenue is cut through the President's Park on the north

1824–25 The park north of the White House is named to honor General Lafayette and planted in a grove according to Bulfinch's design

1825 John Quincy Adams develops the first flower garden and plants ornamental trees

1835 Andrew Jackson creates the White House orangery and adds more trees, including the famous Jackson magnolia

1848 James K. Polk places a statue of Thomas Jefferson on the North Lawn

1850 The noted landscape gardener Andrew Jackson Downing develops a landscape plan for the President's House and the Mall

1853 Clark Mills's equestrian statue of Andrew Jackson is unveiled in the center of Lafayette Park

1853 Under Franklin Pierce the White House orangery is expanded as a greenhouse

1857 The orangery is demolished to make room for a new Treasury wing; a replacement greenhouse is constructed on the west, adjoining the State Floor of the White House

1866, 1871 East and West Executive Avenues are built as public ways on each side of the White House

1867 The wooden greenhouse burns and is replaced by a larger, more nearly fireproof design by Alfred B. Mullett

1870s Julia Grant begins the tradition of White House garden parties and substitutes floral bouquets for social calls; her husband adds a billiard room between the greenhouse and the mansion

1871 Downing's plan for tree planting is initiated; Ulysses S. Grant extends the grounds south beyond Jefferson's stone wall; a great round pool is built on the South Lawn

1873 Another round pool is built on the North Lawn; the Jefferson statue is moved to the Capitol

1878–80 Hundreds of trees are planted under Rutherford B. Hayes, who begins the tradition of commemorative trees to represent each President and state

1870s–1880s The conservatory is expanded to great size, rambling beside and over the West Wing and providing a spring garden for White House residents all year long

1880 The Ellipse south of the White House is completed

1886 The conservatory provides flowers for Grover Cleveland's wedding in the Blue Room

1889 Benjamin Harrison brings the first Christmas tree inside the White House

1902 The conservatory is removed during the White House remodeling by McKim, Mead and White; Edith Roosevelt plants a colonial garden in its place on the west

1913 Ellen Wilson replaces the colonial garden with a formal rose garden designed with George Burnap; the landscape architect Beatrix Farrand designs a new East Garden

1923 Calvin Coolidge places the first National Christmas Tree in Lafayette Park

1935 Franklin D. Roosevelt invites Frederick Law Olmsted Jr. to prepare a plan for the grounds, one that has prevailed

1941 West Executive Avenue is closed to the public for wartime security

1943 Completion of the Jeffersonian Memorial on the Tidal Basin crowns the vista down the South Lawn

1948–52 Harry S. Truman remodels and modernizes the White House, introducing the Truman boxwood across the North Portico

1961 John F. Kennedy has the Rose Garden redesigned to serve presidential functions and places management of the White House garden under the National Park Service

1962–72 The sense of the President's Park is revived when historic buildings surrounding Lafayette Square are preserved and sympathetic new buildings are constructed under the encouragement of Jacqueline Kennedy

1964 Lady Bird Johnson has the East Garden completed in honor of Jacqueline Kennedy

1969 Lady Bird Johnson adds the Children's Garden on the South Lawn

1973 Richard M. Nixon orders a permanent, living Christmas tree planted on the Ellipse

1975 Gerald R. Ford installs the first outdoor swimming pool at the White House

1987 East Executive Avenue is transformed into a pedestrian walkway

1994 Hillary Rodham Clinton inaugurates a temporary display of contemporary sculpture in the East Garden

1995 Pennsylvania Avenue in front of the White House is closed to traffic and new landscaping schemes proliferate

White House Plants

This list indicates some of the flowers, herbs, and trees that have been found at the White House over the years. In the case of many historic plants, exact species are not documented.

HERBACEOUS PLANTS

Aster China aster *Callistephus chinensis;* Stoke's aster *Stokesia laevis*

Autumn crocus *Colchicum* spp.

Black-eyed Susan *Rudbeckia hirta*

Caladium Fancy-leaved caladium *Caladium × hortulanum*

Candytuft Evergreen candytuft *Iberis sempervirens*

Canna *Canna* spp. and hybrids

Carolina jessamine *Gelsemium sempervirens*

Catnip *Nepeta cataria*

Cattail *Typha latifolia*

Chives *Allium schoenoprasum;* Chinese (garlic) chives *A. tuberosum*

Chrysanthemum *Chrysanthemum × morifolium*

Clematis *Clematis* spp. and hybrids

Cockscomb *Celosia cristata*

Coral-bells *Heuchera sanguinea*

Crocus Ankara crocus *Crocus ancyrensis;* cloth-of-gold crocus *C. angustifolius;* Scotch crocus *C. biflorus*

Daffodil *Narcissus* spp.

Dandelion *Taraxacum officinale*

Daylily *Hemerocallis* spp.

Dragonhead *Dracocephalum* spp.

Dusty miller (groundsel) *Senecio vira-vira*

False dragonhead *Physostegia virginiana*

Floss flower *Ageratum petiolatum*

Foxglove *Digitalis* spp.

Gardenia *Gardenia jasminoides*

Geranium *Pelargonium* hybrids

Gladiolus *Gladiolus × hortulanus*

Grape hyacinth *Muscari botryoides*

Heliotrope Common heliotrope *Heliotropium arborescens*

Hollyhock *Alcea rosea*

Honeysuckle *Lonicera* spp. and hybrids

Hosta Siebold hosta *Hosta sieboldiana*

Hyacinth *Hyacinthus orientalis*

Hydrangea Bigleaf hydrangea *Hydrangea macrophylla*

Impatiens *Impatiens wallerana*

Iris *Iris* spp.

Lady's mantle *Alchemilla* spp.

Lady's slipper *Cypripedium* spp.

Lavender *Lavandula* spp.

Lavender cotton *Santolina chamaecyparissus*

Lily *Lilium* spp.

Mint *Mentha* spp.

Mullein *Verbascum* spp.

Oxalis *Oxalis* spp.

Pansy *Viola × Wittrockiana*

Petunia *Petunia* hybrids

Phlox *Phlox* spp.

Pinks Cottage pinks *Dianthus plumarius*

Poinsettia *Euphorbia pulcherrima*

Primrose *Primula* spp. and hybrids

Rose *Rosa* spp. and hybrids

Rosemary *Rosmarinus officinalis*

Sage Blue sage *Salvia azurea;* common scarlet sage *S. splendens;* mealycup sage *S. farinacea;* scarlet sage *S. coccinea*

Strawberry *Fragaria* spp.

Sunflower *Helianthus* spp.

Sweet pea *Lathyrus odoratus*

Sweet William *Dianthus barbatus*

Thyme Common thyme *Thymus vulgaris*

Trumpet vine *Campsis radicans*

Tuberose *Polianthes tuberosa*

Tulip *Tulipa* spp. and hybrids

Water lily *Nymphaea* spp.

Wisteria *Wisteria* spp. and hybrids

Yucca *Yucca* spp.

WOODY PLANTS

Ash Patmore ash *Fraxinus pennsylvanica* 'Patmore'

Azalea *Rhododendron* spp. and hybrids

Beech American beech *Fagus grandifolia*; European beech *F. sylvatica*; fernleaf beech *F. sylvatica* 'Asplenifolia'; purple beech *F. sylvatica* 'Atropunicea'

Bottlebrush buckeye *Aesculus parviflora*

Boxwood Common (American or English) boxwood *Buxus sempervirens*; dwarf boxwood *B. sempervirens* 'Suffruticosa'; Japanese (littleleaf) boxwood *B. microphylla* var. *japonica*

Camellia Common camellia *C. japonica*; sasanqua camellia *C. sasanqua*

Cedar Atlas cedar *Cedrus atlantica*; cedar-of-Lebanon *C. libani*; deodar cedar *C. deodara*; Eastern red cedar *Juniperus virginiana*; Japanese cedar *Cryptomeria japonica*; red cedar *Acrocarpus fraxinifolius*

Cherry Oriental cherry *Prunus serrulata*; Yoshino cherry *P. yedoensis*

Chestnut American chestnut *Castanea dentata*

Coralberry *Ardisia crenata*

Crab apple 'Katherine' crab apple *Malus* 'Katherine'

Dogwood Chinese dogwood *Cornus kousa* var. *chinensis*; flowering dogwood *C. florida*; pink dogwood *C. florida* 'Rubra'; red-twigged dogwood *C. sericea*

Douglas fir *Pseudotsuga menziesii*

Elm American elm *Ulmus americana*; Chinese elm *U. parvifolia*; Dutch elm *U. × hollandica*

Fir *Abies* spp.

Hardy orange *Poncirus trifoliata*

Hawthorn Washington hawthorn *Crataegus phaenopyrum*

Hickory *Carya* spp.

Holly American holly *Ilex opaca*; English holly *I. aquifolium*

Horse chestnut *Aesculus hippocastanum*

Juniper California juniper *Juniperus occidentalis*; common juniper *Juniperus communis*

Lilac *Syringa* spp. and hybrids

Linden American linden *Tilia americana*; littleleaf linden *T. cordata*; pendent silver linden *T. petiolaris*; red-twigged linden *T. platyphyllos* 'Rubra'; silver linden *T. tomentosa*

Magnolia Bigleaf magnolia *Magnolia macrophylla*; saucer magnolia *M. × soulangiana*; Southern magnolia *M. grandiflora*; star magnolia *M. stellata*; white saucer magnolia *M. × soulangiana* 'Alba'

Maple Hornbeam maple *Acer carpinifolium*; Japanese maple *A. palmatum*; Japanese

threadleaf maple *A. palmatum* 'Dissectum'; red maple *A. rubrum*; silver maple *A. saccharinum*; sugar maple *A. saccharum*

Mountain laurel *Kalmia latifolia*

Oak Bur oak *Quercus macrocarpa*; pin oak *Q. palustris*; red oak *Q. rubra*; scarlet oak *Q. coccinea*; white oak *Q. alba*; willow oak *Q. phellos*

Osmanthus Holly osmanthus *Osmanthus heterophyllus*

Palm Crozier cycas *Cycas circinalis*; sago cycas *C. revoluta*

Paulownia (Princess tree) *Paulownia tomentosa*

Pine Eastern white pine *Pinus strobus*; Japanese black pine *P. thunbergiana*

Poplar Lombardy poplar *Populus nigra* 'Italica'

Quince Common quince *Cydonia oblonga*; flowering quince *Chaenomeles speciosa*; Japanese quince *C. japonica*

Redbud Eastern redbud *Cercis canadensis*

Rhododendron Carolina rhododendron *Rhododendron carolinianum*; catawba rhododendron *R. catawbiense*

Sequoia Giant sequoia *Sequoiadendron giganteum*

Spirea Japanese spirea *Spiraea japonica*

Spruce Dwarf Alberta spruce *Picea glauca* var. *albertiana* 'Conica'; Norway spruce *P. abies*

Sycamore Buttonwood (Eastern sycamore) *Platanus occidentalis*

Tulip tree *Liriodendron tulipifera*

Willow Babylon weeping willow *Salix babylonica*; pussy willow *S. discolor*; white willow *S. alba*

Index

Acknowl-
edgments

Opening Illustrations

Page 1: A cast-iron garden settee, purchased in the 1850s by the gardener John Saul for Millard Fillmore, beneath a scarlet oak, left, and a horse chestnut, in the southeast corner of the grounds.
Pages 2–3: The same scene, richly colored by the change to fall.
Pages 4–5: Dwarf boxwood planted in 1952 by Harry S. Truman near the North Portico.
Page 6: Boxwood parterres in the Rose Garden with Fosteriana, Greigii, lily-flowered, and single-late tulips, all shaded by 'Katherine' crab apple and saucer magnolia trees.

A Note on the Sources

This book was written almost entirely from manuscripts and printed documents, a substantial majority of them in the pubic buildings records at the National Archives and the map collections of the Library of Congress. Written materials include letters, reports, invoices, on-the-scene accounts, maps, and proposed and realized plans, as well as Congressional acts and supporting materials. Other written sources are found in presidential and related papers, notably those of Jefferson, Jackson, Grant and his aide General Babcock, Hayes, Theodore and Edith Roosevelt, Franklin D. Roosevelt, and Olmsted Brothers. Another level of research has been accessibility to the White House grounds for study purposes, with the help and advice of those who keep them and know them best.

Acknowledgments

The author extends his appreciation to the following:

For research assistance at the White House, Rex W. Scouten, Chief Curator; Lydia Barker Tederick, Betty C. Monkman, William G. Allman, Donna Hayashi; Dale Haney and Wayne Amos, assistants to Irvin M. Williams, Superintendent of Grounds; Nancy Clarke, Florist; Gary J. Walters, Chief Usher.

Prof. Suzanne L. Turner, Louisiana State University School of Landscape Architecture; Barbara Kirkconnell; Carl A. Ruthstrom; Charles M. Harris.

Rachel Lambert Mellon, for generosity with her collection of historic gardening books and graphics; Julia Blakely and Tony Willis at the Oak Spring Garden Library, Upperville, Va.

Sam Daniel, Library of Congress; John K. VanDereedt, National Archives; T. Michael Miller, Lloyd House Historical Library, Alexandria, Va.; John Rhodehamel, Huntington Library; Sanna Osborne, National Park Service; Gill Gonzales, Rutherford B. Hayes Presidential Center; and Lucinda S. Seale for help with many gardening aspects of the book.

Illustration Credits

All color photographs are by Erik Kvalsvik except as noted.
Sharon Bradley-Papp: 22-23, 74–75, 92; George H. Chittenden: 34 top; Rutherford B. Hayes Presidential Center: 53; Historic American Buildings Survey (Jack E. Boucher): 18, 114; Historical Society of Washington, 51; Huntington Library: 12–13; Library of Congress: 16, 26 top, 52, 54, 55, 56, 64 bottom, 65 bottom, 76, 77, 82, 85 left, 86, 90, 103, 104, 106; Rachel Lambert Mellon Collection, Oak Spring Garden Library, Upperville, Va.: 27, 36, 42, 44, 83; Musée National de la Cooperation Franco-Américane au Château de Blérancourt, © R.M.N.: 34 bottom; National Archives: 37, 38 bottom, 43, 102, 107; National Park Service: 89 right; National Trust for Historic Preservation (Woodrow Wilson House): 65 top; New-York Historical Society: 20, 26 bottom; Philadelphia Museum of Art, Gift of Mrs. Thomas Eakins and Mary Adeline Williams: 112–13; Smithsonian Institution: 38 top; White House Collection: 30–31, 35, 50, 64 top, 85 right, 110–11, 116